Nine Lives

Nine Lives

Memoirs of a Maverick Conservationist

JOHN VARTY

with Dominique le Roux
and Lesley Hay-Whitton

Published by Zebra Press
an imprint of Random House Struik (Pty) Ltd
Reg. No. 1966/003153/07
80 McKenzie Street, Cape Town, 8001
PO Box 1144, Cape Town, 8000 South Africa

www.zebrapress.co.za

First published 2010

1 3 5 7 9 10 8 6 4 2

Publication © Zebra Press 2010
Text © John Varty 2010

Cover photographs © John Varty

PUBLISHER: Marlene Fryer
MANAGING EDITOR: Robert Plummer
EDITOR: Lesley Hay-Whitton
PROOFREADER: Beth Housdon
COVER AND TEXT DESIGNER: Monique Oberholzer
TYPESETTER: Monique van den Berg
INDEXER: Sanet le Roux
PRODUCTION MANAGER: Valerie Kömmer

Set in 11.5 pt on 16.5 pt Adobe Garamond

Printed and bound by Pinetown Printers, Pinetown, KwaZulu-Natal

ISBN 978 1 77022 132 1

Over 50 000 unique African images available to purchase
from our image bank at www.imagesofafrica.co.za

This book is dedicated to Savannah, Sean and Tao.
May you experience the joy, wonder and pleasure
that I have from being close to wild animals.

And to Gill, for giving me three precious gifts
and for sharing in the lives of the big cats.

Contents

Acknowledgements

There are so many people I'd like to thank. Those I miss out, please forgive me.

Firstly, my parents, Boyd and Maidie Varty, who gave me the greatest gift of all – life.

To my partners at Londolozi, Dave Varty and Allan Taylor: thank you for writing the forewords to my book and for supporting me always.

To my partners in Marthly, Doc and Jenny Watson, for great support and friendship.

To the next generation, Bronwyn, Boyd, Savannah, Tao and Sean Varty. To Anton and Kathleen Taylor, and to Pippa, Joey and Roddy Watson, may you work in harmony to carry the spirit of Londolozi forward and may you tread lightly upon her.

To David and Karen Lawrence for guiding us through troubled waters, and for friendship and support.

To Raymond Chasenski, for trying his level best to get me to understand how business works.

To my extended Londolozi family, Chris and Debbie Kane-Berman, Tom and Kate Imrie, Richard and Sarah Ferrier, Bee-Jay Watson, and all the staff of Londolozi, past and present.

To Mo and Kate Grogh, for wonderful advice over the years.

To the rangers, who have always shared their knowledge with me.

To my great tracker and friend, Elmon Mhlongo, and his wife, Agnes. To Renias Mhlongo and Alex van den Heever, who are keeping the art of tracking alive.

To all the trackers I have had the privilege of working with: Winnis Mathebula, Two Tone Sithole, Snotis, Maxim, Kimbyan Mnisi, Judas, Julius Ngwenya, Sandros Mnisi, Richard Siwele and Freddy Ngobeni.

To all the beautiful ladies who work or have worked at Londolozi – I wish I could create one huge harem the way the impala rams do.

To the ladies at the Londolozi booking office, Vida, Linda, Elsje, Didi, Leanne and others – thanks for your support.

To Genene, Dorothy and Salphina, who work so hard to keep me legal.

To Errol Goss, Pierre Marais and Eric Dunn, who have defended me in court. I have no doubt that the truth will be revealed and good will triumph over evil. To Brian Gibson, for advice and support over the years.

To my good friends from the Kruger Park, Dr Roy Bengis, Dr Dewald Keet, Dr Gus Mills, Ian Whyte, Trevor Dearlove, Butch Smuts and John Bassy – thank you for friendship and support.

To Dr Peter Rodgers and Dr Charlotte Moueix for all veterinary support and help.

To my great friends Ian and Moira Thomas, Tony and Dee Adams, Neil and Lynn McLaughlin, Anton and Jo Truesdale, Daryl and Sharna Balfour, Peter and Zaria Lamberti, Ken and

Lynn Maggs, Rodney and Lorna Drew, Jos and Yvette van Bommel, Dave and Miriam Meltzer, James and Trish Marshall, Bruce and Melly Lawson, Oloff Bergh, Dave Salmoni, Tedd Schorman, Marianna Keyser, Mike Myers, Dale McKnight, Liz Westby-Nunn, Chris Badger, Chris Goodman, Emma Kist, Cynzia Carli, Heidi-Lee Stockenström, Gavin Lautenbach, Brett Wallington, Ve Thompson, Claire McDonald, Claire McKechnie, Moz Wolhuter, Susan Anderson, Marieta Wentzel, Lynne Richardson, Susan Baden, Gill and Jacqui Hemphill, Lucien Beaumont, Duncan MacLarty, James and Jess Boom, JC, Claudia, Katja and Tatiana Dubuisson, and James Kydd.

To my extended Cape Town family, Drénie, Mark, Penny, Gerry and Nicky, for friendship and support.

To Phil Fairclough and Peter Lamberti, for restoring my film career.

To Pat Mitchell and Thom Beers for all the support during the days of Turner Original Productions.

To JD and Mary-Susan Clinton for support in financing and selling my films.

To Tedd Schorman, for selling Londolozi films during the years of apartheid.

To my Kenyan partners, Warren and Heather Samuels, Lakakin Sukuli, Karino Sukuli, Moses Onossorran and Leveres Yiamat.

To my Zambian partners, Yusuf and Gulam Patel and General Christian Tembo. To all the game scouts in Luangwa. To Adrian Carr and Sandy Bornman, for giving me Jamu the leopard.

To Karin Slater, whose epic walk saved my life after the helicopter crash, and for great friendship. To Trish Parsons for help and support while Rob and I were in hospital and for her friendship.

To three of nature's great gentlemen, who inspired me: Harry

Kirkman, George Adamson and Norman Carr. George Adamson was the first to show me that it was possible to have a deep and lasting relationship with a big cat.

To Michael and Wendy Hackenberger, for finding Ron and Julie for me.

To Zelda Kobola, who stuck by me through hard and dangerous times during the tiger project.

To all the doctors, homeopaths and traditional healers who restored me to health when I was nearly gone.

To Jann Morrison and Burke Lautenbach, for fantastic support during the tiger project.

To Sunette Fourie, for running my website and doing the bookings for Tiger Canyons, and also for great support and friendship.

To all the people in the Philippolis area who have supported me in the tiger project: Doreen Atkinson and Mark Ingle, Daan and Lettie Pretorius, Abel and Karin Erasmus, GP and Linda van den Heever, Pieter Jacobs, PD Jacobs, Piet Cellier, Piet Simes and Desire van Rensburg.

To Mike Berridge, for wonderful sound recordings and friendship over the years.

To Dominique le Roux for great inspiration and advice.

My thanks go to Marlene Fryer of Zebra Press for having the confidence in me to publish *Nine Lives*.

To Robert Plummer of Zebra Press and Lesley Hay-Whitton, for excellent editorial skills and for correcting and editing my considerable grammatical errors.

To Beth Housdon, Monique Oberholzer, Monique van den Berg, Sanet le Roux and Valerie Kömmer, my sincere thanks for your input, and to Kim Taylor for organising the publicity for *Nine Lives*.

Foreword

My brother John, or JV as he has become known, should have been born a hundred years in the future, into a time when the pursuit of money is no longer the central driving force and the human species has ceased its destructive activities on earth. Life in all its diversity will again be held in high regard and the often fragile links, which interconnect the natural world, will be recognised and held sacred. One hundred years from now it is entirely possible that relationships with wild animals will no longer be regarded as strange and bonds of kinship will be re-established between many of the earth's species.

JV has been at the forefront of such enlightened thinking and, ever since 1969, when he gave up a promising cricket career at the time of the Basil D'Oliveira debacle in South Africa, the natural world has been central to his existence.

As the years have advanced, JV's relationships with the world of nature have become increasingly stronger and profoundly deeper, to the point that he has effectively abandoned the world we know – with its politics, greed, conflict and crime. To me, JV is a messenger sent to us from the future. He implores us to change our ways as he illuminates a future course of action through these dark days of destruction of the natural world. He has used cinematography to shine a light on the magical intelligence and regenerative powers of nature, inspiring the imaginations of young minds, many of whom have aspired to being junior John Vartys. Years later it is those selfsame kids who have chosen to dedicate their careers to the restoration of our Eden.

JV has produced over sixty hours of completed film documentaries, all of which send 'Gaian messages', suggesting to us that we should take greater care of this planet. He has delved deeply into the psyche of animals and has entered into profound emotional relationships with individual big cats, Shingalana the lion being the first, followed by Little Boy and Little Girl and Jamu and all the leopards that shared his space for a while before returning to the wilds.

Almost a decade ago, JV started his great love affair with tigers. The tigers Ron and Julie became the central characters in the two-hour film *Living with Tigers*, and today he regards these two beautiful animals as closer companions than most human friends he has.

In recent times, JV, together with Gillian van Houten, has produced three remarkable and beautiful children. In true JV fashion, he has tackled the project of introducing his youngsters into his world in a single-minded and focused way. While he is a father in the old-fashioned style, consistent and loving, he also expects his children to fit in with his unorthodox lifestyle. His daughter, Savannah, and the boys, Sean and Tao, fill the other part of his life as he and Gillian guide them into adulthood. It says much for his youngsters that they cope with this varied and exciting upbringing.

Nine Lives is an honest account of a remarkable sixty years lived at full tilt. It is a story of a man who surely marches to his own beat and who has the courage of his convictions, spending very little time being his 'social self' and a lot of time being his 'essential self'.

JV has made a wonderful contribution to a growing world consciousness related to the vital role nature plays in all our lives.

It is with great pleasure that I present to you this book. It is different, gripping and inspiring. It is also both serious and fun. Enjoy!

DAVE VARTY, brother and co-owner of Londolozi

Foreword

I am very pleased that John Varty has written this book at long last, as his has been a singularly full and interesting life. I have known him since I was born – our grandfathers bought the game farm Sparta together in 1926, and our parents shared holidays in the old Sparta Hunting Camp.

When we were boys, the four years' difference between John and me elevated him to near god-like status in my mind. He was allowed to carry a .22 rifle, and he knew so much more than I did – I wondered if I'd ever become as skilled in bush craft as John (the answer to that is no).

My father was transferred to Australia, and by the time we returned to Cape Town I was fifteen and Sparta no longer played such an important part in the family's life. At that time the area around Sparta was still used mainly for hunting, and while we did see game, the animals always kept a good distance from us, as they were wary of humans. I enjoyed our visits, but I really wanted to be back in Cape Town where all the girls were – such is the callowness and capriciousness of youth. A relatively minor incident played a part in changing all of that for me.

One evening John came round to our camp in a Land Rover and took us to see lions that were feeding on a zebra. I'd never seen wild lions at close quarters before, and I suddenly saw Sparta through completely different eyes.

It would be wrong to think that it was just the sight of the lions that so affected me. John has always had a way of interesting people in the things close to his heart, and it was his overwhelming enthusiasm that made the greatest impression on me. He had, by that stage, decided to rename Sparta 'Londolozi', and was determined to make it a place where people could experience the wilderness that too few of us are ever exposed to. This was very ambitious at a time when he had no capital and no business plan, and when the land was sorely degraded.

John has always been an unconventional character. His view that, unless wildlife paid for itself, it would disappear, was viewed by many as controversial at best, heretical at worst. He has always been forthright and has spoken out on the issues he believes in, sometimes ruffling the feathers of those who consider themselves great and mighty.

But John had a message that people were waiting and wanting to hear – that it is possible to protect the last remaining wildlife areas, and indeed to return exhausted commercial farms back to productive wilderness areas. He has the ability to enthuse people with his ideas, and to make them want to become a part of whatever project he is currently working on.

For me John's greatest gift is one not necessarily seen by all. When I was going through a time of personal sadness, John suggested that we go and swim in the Sand River, at what we call 'The Waterfall', a very beautiful rapid overhung by ebonies and sycamore figs several kilometres upstream from the Londolozi camps. For an hour and a half we lolled in the swift-flowing water, and he talked to me, telling me of sadnesses he had experienced and joys that had followed, and generally buoying my flagging spirits. John has a quick temper, but his spirit is generous, and never more so than when a friend of his needs sympathy or help. His compassion is great, and this is the quality of his that I admire most.

John has always had a great rapport with children and young people. He was childless for many years, and then had Savannah in his mid-forties, followed by Tao and Sean. I have seen with amusement how this fairly grumpy old bush dog has mellowed as he teaches his children all he knows, how Savannah can wrap him around her little finger, and how his patience never wears thin with the energy and seemingly incessant questioning of the twins.

John is known around the world. His films have reached a global audience, and he and his brother Dave have placed Londolozi's name at the forefront of ecotourism. As you will read in this book, John has had a life filled with many and varied experiences. It is not for me to recount them; I'll leave that up to him. But I must say, in the midst of all his eccentricities, his habit of wading into water to drag dead animals to the bank so he can film the crocodiles feeding on them is, to me, nothing short of lunacy.

John has had many ups and downs in his life, but he has always managed to overcome adversity to press on with his good work. The first few years of the twenty-first century have been extremely gruelling for him owing to external factors, but things have now taken a turn for the better and his star is on the ascendant again. John has been a good friend to me and an excellent business partner. I congratulate him on this fascinating book.

ALLAN TAYLOR, friend and co-owner of Londolozi

Introduction

Somewhere between the terror and sheer exhilaration there must have been a time when life with John Varty was more even-keeled or regular – even with some boring stretches of time, perhaps? Surely? But no, not that I can recall. From the moment my life was joined with his, it became a life of extremes. JV is that kind of man – one that pushes boundaries and lives on the edge.

Take one of my first visits to Londolozi. Fresh from the city and my somewhat designer life as a TV presenter, I was staying at JV's house, dressed that evening in a gauzy, wrap-around little dress, a pair of strappy sandals and a liberal dose of Coco Chanel. We were about to go to the lodge for dinner when the sound of branches snapping in the undergrowth next to the house suggested the presence of elephants.

'Come,' said JV, moving *away* from the safety of the Land Rover and disappearing into the shadows *towards* the sound. 'I can do this,' I resolved, and followed, to find JV crouched low beside a tree trunk, a massive bull elephant looming not ten metres ahead. 'He won't charge, will he?' was about all I could manage from a mouth so dry that my lips were sticking to my teeth. The elephant lifted his trunk and, scenting the air, took one whiff of the Coco Chanel and lunged threateningly closer. All I could see were massive grey wrinkly knees! JV crouched down lower – me, well, I'm not exactly sure what happened, but I found myself hurtling along the path to the house, strappy sandals going one way, me the other as I flew up the stairs and into the bathroom, where I locked the door, the beating of my heart drowning out everything – except what I imagined to be the sound of JV's laughter.

This was to be the tone of my new life, and alarming close-ups of large wild animals became a recurring theme of future years working alongside JV in the bush in different parts of Africa. But, first, two important events took place that were to have far-reaching consequences on our lives. The first was a trip to India to view tigers; the second, the last days and death of the Mother Leopard.

Our tiger safari in India and Nepal was astounding. We spent three months travelling through the reserves in some of the most spectacular jungle and forest habitats, but sadly caught only the occasional glimpse of a tiger, despite endless hours of searching from elephant backs and jeeps. Silently, like a shadow behind the wonder of India, lay the unavoidable truth: Project Tiger – the country's effort to save the tiger – was failing. Then one night, after dinner in our camp at Royal Bardia Park, at the headwaters of the mighty River Ganges, with a full moon rising and the river water crashing through the ravines below, JV said, 'I must try to save the tiger in Africa.'

And he did! This seemingly outrageous comment was to be realised ten years later with the advent of the Tiger Moon ex-situ tiger conservation project in the Karoo.

The Mother Leopard is a Londolozi legend. When I met JV and Elmon, they had been documenting her life on film for twelve years and, realising that her end was near, we spent every possible moment with her in the bush. I came to know her in this, the last year of her life. For me, sitting beside JV in the film vehicle, these were days of wonder. There was a perceptible bond between them, an understanding formed during the many long hours they had spent together, she living her life and JV filming it. To me it was as if there were a silent agreement between them, something much more than a tolerance of each other's presence.

A leopard's life has long periods of not much happening at all. Then, suddenly, as if compressed, all the action – whether it is mating, territorial fighting or hunting – explodes, and for a few wild moments there is a blur of events. The film vehicle hurtles across the bushveld and you hang on white-knuckled as the tyres hit ruts in the road, sending you bouncing clean out of your seat. You duck continually to avoid being struck by thorn branches as they whip back at you, and all the while you try to get your lenses focused to get the shot. JV, more often than not, is cursing, loudly, as inevitably the action happens behind the bush and out of sight. This is why there are few good leopard documentaries. The cameramen who make them have levels of tenacity unknown to other human beings.

When the Mother Leopard died, it was the end of an era. JV was shattered, and from the depths of his grief arose the idea to pay tribute to her by making a feature film about her life. There is nothing moderate about JV's ambitions. As a wildlife film maker, he had mastered the documentary and saw new challenges in a feature film – in this way he would reach a larger audience with the conservation message he was so passionate about.

Hollywood came to Londolozi, trailing the entire retinue of film stars, make-up artists and drama, and with it arrived two tiny leopard cubs, whose ultimate release into the wild (in real life as well) would be the framework of the Mother Leopard's story. As if the implications of raising two leopard cubs weren't enough, as if the feature film wasn't enough of a challenge … out of no-where, something happened that turned all our plans completely upside down.

We rescued an abandoned lion cub in the bush.

Even today I cannot imagine what possessed us to do this; for JV to 'interfere' with nature was completely uncharacteristic. The moment will remain etched in my mind forever, perfectly silent and still – like a freeze frame: sitting in the film vehicle, the sun beating down, the cries of the tiny cub, the thudding of her heart as she lay cupped in my hands. Shingalana. She was with us for three years – the most extraordinary years of our lives, filled with joy, adventure and ultimately the deepest heartache either of us had ever known.

We spent the better part of five years in Zambia at various camps on the Luangwa River in the South Luangwa National Park, filming the release of Little Boy and Little Girl leopard, Shingalana and another leopard cub, Jamu. Life in Zambia was the mother of all rollercoaster rides, giving rise to a catalogue of war stories, from attacks on our camp by a pride of nineteen lions to tsetse fly, malaria, and JV and Elmon's near-fatal helicopter accident.

The South Luangwa is not for sissies, but it is the closest place to Eden I can imagine, untouched as it is by man. Living in simplicity in a tented camp and walking at sunrise and sunset with Shingi or the leopards was other-dimensional and brought us as close as it is possible to blurring the boundary between us and the cats as species. Operating there is of course a logistical nightmare, involving wading through crocodile-infested rivers and hours on rutted tracks if we wanted to go anywhere. Forget fresh fruit and vegetables.

True to what had become the norm, there was plenty of running away from indignant elephant, hippo and buffalo. Cubs are notoriously curious, to the point of being outright cheeky towards animals a hundred times bigger than they are, leaving us to gap it out of uncomfortably close encounters. Actually, it was mostly me doing the ducking; JV was far too busy filming the action. For Elmon, it was always a fine line between loyalty and good common sense.

Hardly a day went by without some major drama – the boat sank with JV in it (this in the crocodile-infested river) and nobody in camp heard him shouting for help. When he finally rescued himself, the air around the camp was blue for days. Despite all these daily difficulties, JV was in his element – everything to him was a challenge, even the 45°C temperatures and maximum humidity, which flattened the rest of us on the team.

It was the helicopter crash that ended our time in Zambia. The birth of our daughter, Savannah, had sent me home to South Africa earlier, and it was only JV's enforced and lengthy recuperations that kept us grounded in South Africa for some time.

Filming in different wildlife areas of Africa felt tame after Zambia, but it was jaw-dropping nevertheless: the spectacle of the migration in Kenya, Savannah tied on my back with a Masai blanket as I photographed; hot showers outside our tent (even if they were from a bucket); bread baked on the coals by our Kenyan chef; and sheets *ironed* by well-trained safari staff. The Kalahari with its russet sand dunes, walking with cheetahs Lozi, Nkosi and Dume, a fiery sun setting. This felt more like what I had signed up for.

The *Out of Africa* idyll was short-lived. Our twin sons were born and not a month later JV arrived home from Canada with two tiger cubs – the pioneers of the tiger project he had conceptualised all those years before in India. The night they arrived, I lay awake in bed wide-eyed, clutching two tiny boys in my arms and listening to the sounds of thudding and crashing as the tiger cubs, Ron and Julie, systematically destroyed our garage.

Having twins is odd enough, but bathing or feeding them and then going for a walk in the bush with two tiger cubs is *bizarre*. And Winnie the Pooh was right: Tiggers do bounce. Life with tigers means being ambushed from all angles and knocked over constantly. Over the years, there have been more bruises and cuts than I can count and more cameras smashed or plunged into the river than any budget can withstand. But being hugged by a tiger remains the most profound experience I know and, in the quiet moments with them, I have seen JV's spirits lift from despair to resolve.

The tiger project is now in its tenth year and has been beset by massive challenges. Most people would have bailed by now, and almost all have. Not JV. He has soldiered on with unparalleled commitment to the tigers. I have always thought that he is the best father a woman could want for her children. The tiger project has shown that he is also the most courageous of people.

GILLIAN VAN HOUTEN

The Hunter

It is dawn in South Africa's lowveld. Reverberating across the bush is the roar of a male lion. A kilometre away, two men and a boy come to a halt. In front is a Shangaan man, a master tracker and hunter named Winnis Mathebula. Behind him stands Boyd Varty, my father, and, behind him, I stand, scared stiff.

Winnis turns his head, listening, pinpointing the exact position of the roaring lion. He turns to my father: 'Xana u dawula?' (Who will be shooting?)

'Nkosana' (The boy), my father replies.

Winnis turns at a right angle to the lion and moves down a game path towards a fallen tree where there is good cover for the three hunters and on which I can rest my rifle. Together we wait, the three of us huddled in the grass behind a round-leaved kiaat bush. I am in front, my father behind me, and Winnis behind him. My father whispers reassuringly into my ear, 'The lion will come down the game path.'

My heart is beating uncontrollably, my hands are shaking and the barrel of the gun is rotating wildly. The lion roars again ... he is coming closer ... fear grips me.

I want to say to my father, 'I'm scared. I don't want to hunt this lion. I want to go home,' but I can't. If I kill this lion, I will pass into manhood; it's a rite of passage, a tradition passed down in the Varty family.

Now is the moment of truth. There is no turning back. I must go through with the hunt. I must show my dad and Winnis that I am brave. I can do it.

The lion appears, walking towards us down the game path, just as my father predicted. He marks his territory and ambles straight towards us. He is totally unaware that he is being watched by three humans lying in wait for him. He is magnificent, with a full black mane … the king.

I squint down the barrel of the gun, lining up the sights on the lion. 'Wait for him to come closer!' my dad commands. The sweat stings my eyes; a fly flicks across my face. I move my hand to brush away the fly and the lion sees the movement; he raises his head. 'Now!' my dad orders, and I shoot the lion through the chest. He drops like a stone.

My dad and Winnis are elated, patting me on the back, shaking my hand. I performed in the heat of the moment – my aim was true and I delivered when it counted most.

I am a man. I am just twelve years old.

In a state of shock and with adrenalin pumping through my body, I move closer to examine the lion. He is in his prime, with a tawny and black mane. A few minutes ago he was roaring, marking his territory, and now he was stretched out, lifeless.

The interaction was brief: we heard him roar and saw him mark territory, he walked towards us and saw us, and I shot him dead. Any chance of our ever meeting again is gone. Any chance of my ever learning anything about the life of this lion is gone.

Instinctively, as I gaze at the magnificent creature, I know something is wrong. What should be the highlight of my young life is tinged with sadness, an inexplicable feeling of loss. I keep it to myself.

All around me is euphoria and celebration. Trackers and hunters arrive. My mother comes out to see the dead lion. The great Harry Kirkman, who is reputed to have hunted and killed over a thousand lions, comes to congratulate me. My status with the Shangaans is sky high; Tilu (my nickname, which means 'thunder and lightning', given to me because of my volatile temper) has killed a lion. I like what I see; I like what I hear.

* * *

My grandfather, Charles Varty, was a businessman and an extremely keen hunter who travelled all around Africa, hunting. He was very friendly with James Stevenson-Hamilton, the first warden of the Kruger National Park. In 1926, he and his business partner, Frank Unger, an equally enthusiastic hunter, were playing tennis in Johannesburg when they heard that some land just outside the Kruger National Park was up for sale. A map was delivered to them at the tennis party, on which the available land was demarcated. They decided then and there to buy two pieces of land, sight unseen, with a total area of 4 000 morgen (about 3 400 hectares), paying one shilling and sixpence per morgen.

They divided the land between them, and my grandfather drove in his car to the village of White River in today's Mpumalanga province, where he hired a span of oxen and a team of porters. Guided by his map and a compass, he headed for the Sand River, which was part of the land he'd bought. He planned to make his camp there.

After weeks of trekking, the porters just sat down. They went on strike, declaring that there was no river and refusing to budge. Charles, who was a skilled linguist, used his very best Zulu and the offer of more money to try to persuade them to go on. Finally, after much bargaining, they agreed to continue and, just a few hundred metres further on, they found the river. The point where he reached the river is exactly where the Londolozi camp is situated today.

* * *

My father, Boyd, used to tell me another story about his father. When my dad was a little boy, he and his father were travelling in the ox wagon. They had been delayed on their journey and it was getting late. My grandfather knew that it wasn't a good idea to pitch their tent in the dark, but he wanted to cross over a small river to pitch his camp on the other side. Although it wasn't yet dark, the sun was starting to set, so he was under some pressure.

As they went down into the river bed, a male lion reared up and grabbed the front ox. The lion had been watching them from the reeds, waiting for his opportunity. Since the light wasn't great by this time, my grandfather couldn't see well enough to take a shot, so he shouted to my dad, 'Bring the light! Bring the light!' My father lit his father's front and back sights with the paraffin lantern, and my grandfather could get the bead on the lion to shoot it.

* * *

My grandfather contracted pneumonia while doing what he loved – hunting – and he died at the age of sixty-five. My own dad fell asleep while he was hunting with friends and never woke up; he was fifty-five.

There is no doubt that hunting ran deep in the veins of the Varty men, and it was in this environment, surrounded by the love for hunting, that I grew up. We were not taught conservation in those days, just hunting. We were taught to hunt ethically – to shoot only the males; never to shoot from a vehicle; and so on. The training that I received from my father and Harry Kirkman, who also took me out hunting with him, stood me in good stead when I started working with big cats later in my life.

I went to school in Johannesburg, and every holiday our family would go to our game farm, Sparta. The whole holiday would revolve around hunting.

There was a saying in the family that the guns took preference over everything else. My dad owned twenty-six of them, and he was a perfectionist about them. It was my job to help him keep them clean, and I mean clean! It was absolutely inexcusable to have a dirty gun.

There were four mud huts at Sparta, all facing inwards, for safety, towards a wood fire on which we used to cook our food. One of the mud huts was used as the gun hut in those days. Before we were allowed to eat, Dad would lay each of the guns out in its allocated slot. He would give me eight guns to clean aside from my own one, and when my little brother, Dave, was old enough, he'd give him four to clean. Dad would inspect every single gun closely after it had been cleaned.

All that mattered in those days was Dad's supply of beer and the guns. The food, which Mom took care of, and everything else, was irrelevant.

We used to hunt impala or wildebeest to provide the camp with meat. We would set out early in the morning, before it was light, and drive to a dry river bed where the road ended. This area was reserved for hunting, and from there we'd continue on foot. By this time, the sun would be coming up and Winnis would start looking for fresh tracks for us to follow. If we heard a lion roaring, Winnis would listen carefully and sometimes say, 'No, no, those are females calling. I haven't heard a male.' We wouldn't follow those sounds, because we weren't allowed to hunt lionesses.

My dad was close friends with Winnis, who featured prominently in every hunting story that Dad told. His admiration for Winnis's tracking skills and bush craft was huge. I personally believe that there was no human being on earth that my father admired more than Winnis Mathebula.

Winnis was quite an entertainer as well as a master of the moment. When we were tracking lions, Winnis would stop and silently and deliberately load his shotgun. For those behind him, this was the signal that we were getting close ... very close! I can remember the excitement and the unbelievable tension I felt as a kid when Winnis loaded his shotgun.

Winnis was one of the very few people my dad trusted alone with me in the bush. One day, when I was carrying my .22 rifle, we trapped a troop of monkeys in a tree. My box of bullets was half-full, which meant there were twenty-five bullets left. I fired all twenty-five remaining bullets, but I missed every single one. Undeterred, the faithful Winnis ran back to camp to fetch more bullets, but as soon as he was gone the monkeys came down the tree and ran away.

When I was ten years old, my father allowed me to go and

stay with Harry Kirkman, who was then warden of Sabi Sand Reserve. The game reserve had been pioneered by my grandfather and Frank Unger and consisted of a consortium of game farms that included Sparta. Harry Kirkman had worked in the Kruger National Park as a game ranger under the park's then warden, James Stevenson-Hamilton. Harry was famous across the lowveld for his fearlessness and because he could shoot faster and more accurately than anyone else.

Harry's Shangaan name was Mlilwana, which means 'little fires'. He was named so because his eyebrows looked like fires burning through the grass, and because his temper was quick and fierce.

My father was a sport hunter. He believed in fair chase: going out on your own two feet without telescopic sights, and out-witting the game. When it came to predators, you shot only the male. Conversely, Harry Kirkman's approach had been moulded by James Stevenson-Hamilton. When Stevenson-Hamilton started Kruger early in the twentieth century, there were few game animals in the reserve, as they had been hunted out. He reasoned that, if he reduced the populations of predators, such as lions, leopards, hyenas and wild dogs, the number of prey animals would increase. Harry's policy was the same. He was the warden for the whole area, including Sparta, and he shot everything – male, female, big, small. Anything carnivorous was fair game. I remember being with him once when an entire clan of hyenas was wiped out.

So Harry tried to build up the game animals by taking the number of carnivores down. We know today that nature doesn't work that way. If an animal's numbers are declining you have to look to the habitat. At the moment the blue wildebeest is on the decline at Londolozi and we know that the problem lies with its habitat.

When I went hunting with Harry, he taught me that, if I wanted to be a successful hunter, it was no good taking aim deliberately, as this took too much time. He showed me how to bring the gun to my shoulder quickly, to take instinctive aim and to fire. He showed me where to place the vital shots and the angles at which the bullets would travel. It was all about confidence, and Harry had plenty of it. Fearless and confident, Harry was my hero, my role model. I was determined to emulate him.

Often when we were out hunting together he'd say to me, 'You do the shooting.' He was in his sixties by then and had shot over a thousand lions. He'd had enough of shooting. So I would shoot the hyenas and the wild dogs – any predators we encountered.

Another thrilling activity with Harry was the anti-poaching patrols. When the game scouts reported that they had located wire snares, Harry would take me along and we would wait for the poachers to return to their snares.

A wire snare is a loop made from strong wire or cable, which is secured to a tree with a loop placed at head height. The snare would be laid on a game path, often near a water hole. When an antelope came down the path to drink, it would inadvertently walk into the noose, which would tighten around its head and throat. As the antelope fought to free itself, the noose would tighten further, choking it to death.

The poachers were poor Shangaan people who lived outside the park. They would set snares in the hope of catching an antelope for the meat, which they would use to feed their families.

The poachers called the wire snare 'the silent gun' because it could kill silently and effectively.

The problem with the wire snare was that it was indiscriminate. I have seen lions, leopards, elephants and hippos wandering around with infected wire-snare wounds that have caused excruciating pain and suffering to the unfortunate animal.

Each of the farms on the Sabi Sand Reserve had game scouts, and six of the best scouts worked under Harry, the warden. Winnis was the game scout for Sparta. Once a month, Winnis would report to Harry about snares he'd found. On full-moon nights, Harry and the game scouts would stake out the snares, forming a circle hidden in the grass. The guys had sticks that they would tap if they saw a poacher. Then they would all rush the snares, hoping to catch him. Harry would often end up catching his own game scouts, who were themselves also poaching.

Although this was exhilarating, it was frequently dangerous, as the poachers were armed – in the old days they often had bows and arrows, and many of them carried spears and pangas (machetes), and even old muskets and rifles. The poachers knew they would be sent to jail if they were captured and they could turn violent if they were caught. One night, while Harry was trying to handcuff a poacher he'd caught, the poacher turned on him, slashing him with a panga, before getting away.

On another occasion, I was lying in the circle waiting for the poachers when, to my right, silhouetted against the moon, I saw a man with a large beard staring towards the position of the snares. After a while he turned and melted back into the night. No other poachers came that evening.

Years later, I was working in the dark with an outstanding

tracker called Two Tone Sithole. I saw Two Tone silhouetted against a spotlight and recognised the beard immediately. I asked him about the poaching incident and he admitted that it had been him I had seen that night. 'How did you know we were waiting for you?' I asked.

'I smelt you,' he replied.

'So you are a poacher?' I asked him.

'No, I'm not,' he retorted. 'Neither you nor Harry Kirkman, nor anyone else, has ever caught me. I have no criminal record.'

Later I would hunt my first leopard with Two Tone Sithole, an incident that is described later in this book. Two Tone went on to track many lions and leopards for tourists to photograph, although he could never see the point in tracking an animal for hours if we weren't going to shoot it.

It is a tribute to my dad that he allowed his son at such an early age to spend so much time with Harry Kirkman. My father had been invited by James Stevenson-Hamilton to be a ranger in the Kruger National Park, but his father, Charles, had insisted that he go to university and follow a 'proper' career – in mining. Harry led the kind of life my father would like to have led. My father, who never really adapted to city life, enabled me to have the freedom that he hadn't been allowed himself. I will be forever grateful to my father for this privilege and to Harry Kirkman for teaching me so much about the bush.

Harry was a legend and when, in the course of his rounds, he visited the farms that made up Sabi Sand Reserve, the owners would offer him a gin and beg him to tell them one of his stories. He couldn't tell stories on demand, so invariably he would refuse. But when he and I were out on patrol together and lying in our sleeping bags next to the camp fire, looking up at the night sky, Harry would tell me his amazing stories. And then he would say to me, 'JV, now you keep that story to yourself; don't tell anyone, understand?'

'I understand,' I would reply. One story Harry did allow me to tell, however, was the story about the only lion that had ever caught him. This is his story.

Two guys had come as guests to one of the Sabi Sand game farms to hunt. A male lion came into the camp one evening as the light was fading and one of these guys took a shot at the lion, wounding him. The lion ran off. When you wound a lion, you are required to report it to the warden, which they did.

The next morning Harry followed the lion's blood trail with his game scout, taking the two hunters with him. Harry knew from many years' experience of hunting lions that a lion would always growl before charging and, in the split second after hearing the growl, he would have time to take aim and fire.

This one didn't growl. Without any warning, the lion sprang. Harry swung his rifle up to break the charge, and the strap caught in the reeds. He pulled at the strap to free the gun and the strap broke. The force jerked the rifle in the wrong direction, so that it was pointing up in the air, and in that second the lion bit hard into Harry's hand. The hunters, who were afraid of shooting Harry, shot into the lion's back, and the wounded lion once again ran off.

Harry Kirkman was known for his fearlessness ... some might even say recklessness. He had tangled with this lion and he was determined to go after it. Other people would have gone back for reinforcements or a pack of dogs; some might have gone to hospital to get their mauled hand seen to. Not Harry. Harry knew that he was dealing with an unusually cunning lion, a lion that had doubled back on its tracks and lain in wait for them behind a rock. He was determined to shoot it.

Harry and his game scout and the hunters picked up the trail again. After they had followed it for some time, the trail led them to a rocky outcrop, at which point it disappeared. Harry climbed onto a high rock but still he couldn't see the trail, so he guessed that the lion had pulled the same trick and doubled back on its trail again. Harry followed suit and backtracked, going right around to the high ground. From there he could see the lion waiting for him in the reeds. Supporting his gun on his injured hand, he and the hunters shot and killed the lion.

* * *

Harry had married a woman who already had children, and he never had any of his own. His wife, Ruby, was a real lady. She had some sort of skin complaint and wore white gloves all the time. She was always immaculately turned out, with a big hat and a long, fashionable cigarette holder. She looked after us when we went to the house and she was very fond of me. She used to tell me about the time she had killed a lion herself. But we didn't go to the house very often. Harry spent most of his time in the bush, and it was a lonely life, living in tents for months and months at a stretch. He had contracted malaria many times and I have heard that quinine, which was the only treatment for the illness available in those days, could cause sterility in men.

One evening while we were out on patrol, we were sitting around the camp fire and he said to me, 'JV, kom hier' (JV, come here). I went over to him and he told me very seriously, 'Be careful that when you marry you don't end up supporting someone else's children.'

I asked him if he would like to have had his own child.

He replied, 'Yes, very, very much so, and I would like to have had a son like you.' He was quite emotional when he said it.

This was the greatest compliment he could have paid me.

When later I came to rehabilitate dangerous cats into the African bush, the skills that Harry Kirkman taught me were the finest training anyone could wish to have had.

2

The Professional Cricketer

When I was at school at Parktown Boys' High in Johannesburg, I generally went to school only for about three days a week, on sporting days. My parents would drop me at school in the car, and I'd jump on my motorbike to go and practise cricket and tennis. I did some schoolwork in between the sport, but it really wasn't important to me.

I excelled at both cricket and tennis. Within my family, there was an ongoing feud – my father wanted me to go on to play cricket professionally, while my mother wanted me to play tennis.

My father, Boyd, had had rheumatic fever as a child, which was quite serious in those days, and it had left him with a weak heart. As a result, he wasn't very strong and he wasn't a good runner. When he played cricket, he was the wicketkeeper, as this position didn't involve too much running. He was never more than an average cricket player, but cricket was always his passion and he followed it avidly. So he was keen for me to excel as he hadn't been able to.

Maidie Varty (née Hellier), my mother, was born in 1919 in Yeoville, Johannesburg. She was an only child in a poor family, and had a very promising tennis career. In 1938 she was chosen to play juniors at Wimbledon, and my father went along to watch her play. The outbreak of World War II the following year, however, put an end to her tennis career. When the war ended, she was too old to compete at that level. She and my father had married by then anyway. My sister, Claudia, was born a couple of years after the war was over, I was born three years later and my brother, Dave, four years after me.

My mother focused all her energy and passion for tennis on me, taking me around the country to play in junior tennis tournaments. I also remember being a ball boy for great tennis players such as Rod Laver, Lew Hoad and Ken Rosewall. Could it be possible, I thought at the time, that one day I too could be a professional tennis player?

I loved cricket *and* tennis, and my parents each believed that I would play for South Africa in their own sport. I believe both of them would have been proud of me if I'd excelled at either one of the sports.

I was highly competitive and losing was not on my agenda – I played to win. In 1966 I was selected to play for the Transvaal Nuffield cricket team, and I became captain in 1968. The same year I was selected to play for the South African Schools cricket team; it was one of the proudest moments of my life and that of my parents.

The South African Schools team gets to play against the host province's team, and that particular year we had to play against Natal. The Natal team was powerful, boasting among its ranks Barry Richards, Vince van der Bijl, Pat Trimborn and Lee Irvine, all Springbok greats.

The wicket was green and seam bowler Vince van der Bijl was almost unplayable on the grassy wicket. I was due to bat fourth, and it wasn't long before I was sent in to face the music.

As Barry Richards walked past me, he said, 'Get onto the back foot, play late and don't commit.' I took his advice and managed to score about 50 runs (out of a total 120 or so) for the schoolboys. As I walked off the field, a man approached me: Would I like to play professional cricket in England, he asked. Without hesitation I answered, 'Yes'.

Norman Featherstone and Tich Smith, whom I played with on the South African Schools team, travelled overseas to play professional cricket with huge success, as did other guys that I played with over the years, such as Clive Rice, Lee Irvine and Allan Lamb. Many regarded professional cricket as a stepping stone to becoming a Springbok cricketer.

I talked it over with my father and mother and they both agreed that I should go to England to play professional cricket. From there I would try to make the senior Springbok cricket team, which was the ultimate in any South African cricketer's career.

There was just one problem: first I had to do my compulsory military training for one whole year.

I was drafted into the air force, where I rose to the rank of second lieutenant, and I was selected to play for the South African Defence Force cricket team. All was going according to plan for me to become a professional – and one day a Springbok – cricketer. The year was 1968.

On 30 August that year, an officer brought me the tragic news that my father had died in his sleep while on a hunting trip with friends and that I needed to go home. It was a devastating blow. My rock, my anchor, my role model, my mentor, my father, my friend was gone. He was just fifty-five and I was eighteen years old.

I was given compassionate leave and I drove home. The first person I saw when I got there was my mother, who was also in a state of deep shock. The guys my father had been hunting with came around to the house, bringing his guns and clothes, and they told us what had happened.

They were sitting around the camp fire after a day's hunting. On doctor's orders, my father was drinking Tab (diet cola). It was a cold winter's night, so he turned in early, climbing into his sleeping bag in his truck. He was always the first up, very early in the mornings, and he would wake the others. Around seven o'clock the next morning, his friends got up and made the fire, thinking that my father must have gone for a walk. Then they saw that he was still sleeping. Normally they would have been out hunting already by this time, and they thought it was funny that the early riser was still asleep. When they shook him, he didn't respond, and they realised with shock that he was dead.

My father hadn't suffered at all, but had slipped away peacefully in his sleep. He was out hunting, around the camp fire with friends, doing something he loved, which is not a bad way to go.

As my father's estate was being wound up, my mother was advised by the trustee of the estate to sell Sparta and invest the money to pay for her children's education.

When she told me that she had been advised to sell the family farm, it was as if a rocket had hit me. I said to her on the spot, without thinking twice, 'I will sacrifice my cricket – I will sacrifice everything – but I will never, ever allow the land to be sold.'

My mother asked me how I was planning to make a living out of wildlife, and I told her to look at Loring Rattray, our neighbour, who had started the internationally successful Mala Mala game reserve. 'We can run safaris the way he does,' I said.

'Yes,' she replied, 'but Loring is a multimillionaire. You're just a boy from a working-class background.'

I told her that what we had at Sparta couldn't be bought with money and that Dad would not have wanted us to sell it.

That made her think.

All she said was, 'All right, I will back you and Dave. You go and start your safaris, but on one condition: you must complete your university career. You have to finish your university degree, and once you've got that degree, you can go and try your safaris and see if you can make some money out of them.'

I didn't realise it fully at the time, but the day my father died was the day my dream of playing professional cricket and representing South Africa in the sport died too. This was a defining moment in my life, which changed dramatically, turning in a totally new direction.

3

Londolozi Is Born

The days immediately after my father's death are blurred and confused in my mind. I can recall little of what happened. I disappeared into a directionless vacuum.

My one aim in life was to support my mother, Maidie, who, like me, was devastated by my dad's death.

My parents had very different temperaments but they were devoted to each other. My father was introverted, straightforward, very private and generous to a fault. His world revolved around his wife, his children and his game farm, Sparta. Somebody had once asked him why the roads on Sparta were so bad, and he'd replied, 'If the roads are bad, nobody will come to visit me.'

My mother, by contrast, was extroverted and gregarious. She loved going out to the theatre in town, but my dad would always stay at home. She had the rare ability to make friends with kings and queens and peasants alike.

These two wonderful people were supportive parents who gave generously of their time, which is ultimately the most important thing you can give to a child. They came to cheer me on at every cricket and tennis match I played when I was at school. Their influences and their wisdom are always with me, and I tell my own children, 'The time on earth with your parents is precious; value every moment. Your family is the most important team you will ever play in.'

If my father had lived to seventy or eighty, instead of dying at fifty-five, he would have kept Sparta as a private hunting farm and my life would have turned out very differently.

After his death, I finished my military training and then, at my mother's insistence, I went to the University of the Witwatersrand to get a Bachelor of Commerce degree ... although what I know about business even today can be written on a postage stamp. The Vartys have never been good businessmen, but we are pioneers; we are always embarking on ambitious projects that have never been tried by anyone else before – but we aren't particularly good at backing them up with business sense!

When my studies were over, I needed to find a way to earn some money. Loring Rattray, our neighbour, had started operating safaris on his farm Mala Mala in the late 1960s. I decided that we could do something similar to what he was doing. His circumstances were very different from ours, however – he was very wealthy and owned a lot of land, with a fancy camp. We had no money and a few small mud huts! All we had in our favour was the optimism of youth.

One day, in 1973, I was in a prefabricated hut on Sparta, sitting in a cardboard box; it was meant to serve as our chair but it wasn't strong enough to sit on, so I was inside it. I remember thinking to myself that I had thrown away a professional cricket career with the promise of a good salary and a house and a car, and here I was sitting in a cardboard box, with nothing.

A commercial airline had offered to fly me out every weekend from Sparta to play cricket, but this arrangement could not have worked – the guests we had at that time came on weekends only and I had to be at the farm to take care of them. South Africa had also been thrown out of international cricket at that stage, so the chances of my becoming a Springbok cricket player were non-existent. There were no South African Test cricketers during that period. But even if this had not been the case, my cricket career had ended when my father died, and I needed to devote myself to the game farm.

So I was idly flicking through a Zulu dictionary, sitting in my cardboard box, when I saw the word 'londolozi' ('the protector'). I said to my brother, Dave, 'Let's call Sparta Londolozi and start photographic safaris.'

Dave agreed, and so began a rollercoaster ride of people, land, wild animals and wonder. We started with a lot of enthusiasm and many ideas, but no business plan, experience or money.

Dave, who is four years younger than I, is more disciplined, better organised and more conventional than I am. His organisational skills are incredible, and his passion and enthusiasm are infectious. No one could have wished for a better partner.

My other partner at Londolozi is Allan Taylor, who is the grandson of Frank Unger, my grandfather Charles Varty's business partner and the son of Elizabeth Taylor. He inherited the other half of the game farm Sparta.

Allan's mother had spoken out strongly against the hunting of lions. She was ahead of her time, and it was a great joy to her when Sparta became Londolozi and hunting turned to photography.

Allan has been an amazing partner to Dave and me. He has

never lived at Londolozi but has played a supportive role in the running of it and has attended all the board meetings. He has remained loyal and steadfast in the face of adversity, backing us in times of crisis, of which there have been several. The Varty family has received much of the credit for Londolozi, but none of it would have been possible without Allan Taylor. Our partnership is held together by the shake of a hand. Long may it last.

* * *

Londolozi lies in South Africa's lowveld, west of the Kruger National Park, and forms part of the Sabi Sand Reserve, one of the biggest private game reserves in the world. When we started Londolozi, the bush was thick, with bad gulley erosion. Wild dogs lived in other game reserves, where the bush wasn't so dense. While there were lions and leopards at Londolozi, they were shy and extremely difficult to find. Wildebeest, zebra and waterbuck were declining – anything that relied on grass was vanishing.

Never short of good ideas or enthusiasm, in 1974 we started luxury, wilderness, walking and canoeing safaris. Talk about trying to capture every niche in the market at once!

The first guinea pigs in our attempt at luxury safaris were some business people from overseas who were being hosted by friends of my mother's. We decided to treat them like royalty, so we chartered two planes to fly them in to the airstrip at Mala Mala. We picked them up in our very best jeeps, which were still rather rickety, and took them on a game drive in Londolozi … but we could find hardly any game – certainly nothing like the lions and leopards they were expecting to see.

Our four mud huts were far too rough for them to stay in, so after the game drive the planes were there to fly them to a hotel in the small town of Hazyview, where they would have a good meal and spend the night. The first plane landed on the hotel runway, but the second pilot decided it wasn't safe to land, as a storm had come up.

We were just relaxing in camp after the game drive when the plane returned, flying very low over our camp and landing at Mala Mala. We guessed that something must have gone wrong, so we shot down there to pick up the guests in this plane and bring them back to our humble camp.

The storm had moved in over our camp by this time, and we realised we would have to feed our guests. Our Shangaan cook did his best to produce a luxury meal – the first ever at Londo-lozi, dished up on our very basic plastic crockery – and, just as it was served, the storm cleared and a swarm of stink bugs invaded the food. The meal was inedible; it was a complete disaster. The plane couldn't fly at night, so we had to drive the guests to Hazyview. They were all dead quiet in the jeeps throughout the hour-and-a-half journey. We finally delivered them to their hotel around midnight, cold and hungry.

The next morning, the two planes brought them back for a game drive, but all we saw this time were two duikers, four impalas and one crippled giraffe. At the end of this 'luxury safari', the planes took them back to Johannesburg.

My mom phoned later that day to ask how it had gone. When I told her what had happened, in typical Maidie Varty style she replied, 'Well, then, you will refund them every single cent they have paid.' So we refunded them all the princely sum of eight rand, which they had each paid!

Next we tried canoe safaris with a bunch of guys and girls from Johannesburg, who paid five rand each. The Sand River, which runs through Londolozi, was in flood and moving fast, and none of us was a skilled canoeist. Within a few minutes, one of the canoes hit a rock under the water and its occupants fell out. We carried on for another 200 metres, and then one of the canoes hit a hippo bull. The guy in it grabbed a branch to try to avoid the enraged hippo. He was left hanging from the branch as the canoe carried on down the river, and he ended up falling into the water. He managed to escape the hippo. The river has shallow rapids, so we carried the canoes more than we paddled them, getting scratched in the reeds. After travelling for about a kilometre, we gave it up as a bad job. In the course of this safari, one of the guys lost his glasses in the river, someone else lost his camera and another guy lost his binoculars. Everyone in the party was lacerated, and one guy had a badly twisted ankle.

We pulled the plug on our canoeing safaris after just one attempt. It had seemed like a good idea at the time, but it just wasn't practical. We realised subsequently that the Sand is the least navigable river in the whole country because of all its rapids. The only time you can really canoe on it is when it's in flood, but that's also the most dangerous time.

Our rough safaris proved a winner. The guests had iron beds with cork mattresses to sleep on. The four mud huts, which we inherited from Dad's hunting days, had bugs in the roof that regularly dropped onto guests in the middle of the night. There were drop toilets, and the shower was a pipe in a tree outside.

Guests brought their own food, and for this rough safari adventure we charged three rand per person per night slept. Once, one guest stayed up drinking the whole night and suggested that, because he hadn't slept, he didn't have to pay the three rand! A year later, after much deliberation, we increased the price to eight rand per person per day.

On one occasion the entire safari was rained out – all the guests saw was one white rhino running away in the rain. Dejected, we refunded the guests their money.

The wilderness safaris were another huge success. Ian Player, a former ranger for Natal Parks Board, had pioneered the wilderness concept as early as the fifties in the then Umfolozi Game Reserve. During his Wilderness Leadership Schools, which continue to this day, young disciples go out into the wilderness for four days, walking from camp to camp, studying beetles and dung and tracks.

The idea behind the wilderness schools was to expose young people to a wilderness experience over the course of four days and then to try to convert them to the cause of helping to save our dwindling wildlands. It is almost a religious experience, as the disciples contemplate the wilderness and then go out to try to convert others to the wilderness movement.

It is a tribute to Ian Player's vision that the wilderness movement survives today and that tens of thousands of people have passed through and been inspired by the wilderness in which they've spent time.

The Wilderness Education Trust was a splinter group made up of businessmen who had gone on a wilderness trail and been inspired to start their own movement. They came to Londolozi and helped us get our wilderness safaris off the ground.

Our wilderness safaris were less serious than Ian Player's, focusing more on learning through having fun. Instead of taking youngsters out in the heat of the day, I would take them on game drives at night, with spotlights to see nocturnal animals, and we'd sit around camp fires with lots of singing and dancing and telling stories.

Through the Wilderness Education Trust, a wide variety of kids came on these safaris. I found the experience absolutely fascinating.

One week I'd take out a group of privileged kids from the poshest schools in Johannesburg. They had no idea how to build a fire or get their sleeping bags out, let alone cook a meal or put a stretcher up. When they finally prepared the meal on one occasion, one girl burnt herself and dropped the pot, so they went to bed hungry that night. They knew a lot about wildlife and ecology and would come up with really intellectual questions, but in practical terms they were a disaster.

The next week I'd take out a group of boys from the private childcare organisation Boys' Town, who had a definite hierarchy: I would give them chores and the big boys would make the smaller boys do them. They were smart kids when it came to practical stuff and they had the camp organised in minutes.

The next week I'd be taking disadvantaged kids from really poor backgrounds out; the following week it would be deaf kids.

The Wilderness Education Trust and I didn't always see eye to eye on how the safaris should be run. As businessmen, the members of the trust wanted to formalise everything and prescribe the number of hours' training we would give the kids. This didn't work for me. One time I was leading a group of teenage girls from a convent and the temperature was around 38°C. I drove them down to the river, stripped off my clothes and climbed into the water. Next thing six of the girls followed suit. The guy from the Wilderness Education Trust was not happy and sat sulking under a tree in his khaki clothes. According to him, this was not what the wilderness safari was supposed to be about; I should have been giving the girls a serious lecture in that heat. He told me he was going to report me to the Wilderness Education Trust.

Two Tone Sithole did a great tracking job on game drives with these girls from the convent – we saw leopard and lion, which was unheard of in those days. I taught them what I could and allowed them to let their hair down, which they enjoyed as a break from their strict convent life.

The guy in the khaki suit went back and filed a report, and I received a letter saying that this was not what the Wilderness Education Trust had in mind. And so ended three fun-filled years of guiding kids on wilderness safaris.

From my perspective, I knew that if the kids were having fun they were more likely to become 'wilderness ambassadors'. The wilderness purists didn't like the concept, but we had a lot of fun on our trails, and many of the kids I took out have stayed in touch with me, saying it changed the direction of their lives.

One young man phoned me up and told me that he had come on a Londolozi wilderness trail when he was fourteen years old. On the trail I had given a lecture on how wildlife was more efficient than domestic stock in the low rainfall regions of Africa. He was now twenty-four years old and had inherited his father's cattle farms in the Waterberg region of Limpopo province. He had got rid of the cattle, and only wildlife roamed the ranches. The talk I had given on the wilderness trail had inspired him to make the change.

In the late seventies I was determined to find out how the Londolozi habitat worked and why we couldn't find game (apart from duiker, impala and bushbuck, which can cope with dense bush) on our land. In the course of this, I attended several conferences, where I met maverick ecologist Ken Tinley. He came to Londolozi and taught us how to change the balance between the grasslands and the woodlands. He told us that if we had wild animals we should photograph them, hunt them *and* eat them. He showed us how to share the land with the people that live around Londolozi so that they can benefit from the wildlife as well – the idea being that if you make the land productive you can feed the people. Another thing we learnt from him was the notion of taking a poacher and turning him into a tracker. We went on to become close friends.

Using a bulldozer, we cleared the trees where the land had eroded due to overgrazing. This raised the water table and, as a result, grass grew. We now have phenomenal grasslands at Londolozi, which means that the visibility is good and the grazer species have returned and are on the increase. When you build up game and there is plenty of water, the predators return. We have herds of zebra, elephant and buffalo 600 strong, as well as prides of lion, leopard and cheetah. Coalitions of male lions patrol the area. Wild dogs have denned on Londolozi over the last three years, and we have packs of spotted hyena.

The increase in predator species has given us a huge amount of insight into inter-predator relationships.

I did the original training in land management myself and have passed on my training methods to all the guys at Londolozi.

No ranger is allowed behind the wheel of one of our jeeps unless he has embraced the Londolozi Model.

Our culture and ethic go like this: take care of the land, take care of the people, take care of the wildlife.

Over time, Londolozi has evolved and changed. We have received numerous awards over the years. From our humble, stink-bug-infested beginnings, we now offer Relais & Châteaux–standard food and our accommodation is world-class, but it is once again a family-run business. We've created a living model that involves the people and improves the land.

4

The Good Companion

When we started Londolozi in 1973, Dave, my younger brother, still had to do his compulsory military training. I needed someone to help me get the business off the ground, and a good friend of mine, Howard Mackie (Mac), came to mind. Both our fathers had been involved in mining, and Mac and I had been friends since childhood, when our families used to go on holiday together to Lake Kariba in what was then Rhodesia.

Mac's passion was fast cars and his dream was to be a Formula 1 racing driver. He had been expelled from school and had dropped out of university. He never seemed to finish anything, and at that stage he was drifting around aimlessly. So I said to him, 'Mac, you are at a loose end. Do you want to come and help me?' And he said yes.

Mac was great company. He was an intelligent, offbeat guy who knew absolutely nothing about the bush or hunting. He lived life to the full, smoking, drinking and partying hard. He was an avid reader who wrote poetry in his spare time (of which there was a lot, because he believed in 'play first, work second').

Mac had an inventive way of looking at life. One day he walked into our pantry, which was a little mud hut with some planks for shelves. Pulling deeply on his cigarette, he said, 'JV, the beer has run out and we've got nineteen tubs of margarine!'

James Dean was a hero of his, and he lived by the motto, 'Live fast, die young and have a good-looking corpse'. Mac was impulsive, and terrible with money – on one occasion I sent him off to town with R400 to buy supplies; he returned with a puppy and no supplies, and on top of it all he'd lost his passport.

He was good-looking and charismatic, with long hair and scruffy clothes (even worse than mine). I'd get up in the morning, take off the tracksuit I'd slept in, put on my bush clothes and go to work. Mac would get out of bed, put on my discarded tracksuit and go to work.

Conditions were rough in those early days at Londolozi. Our guests would have to bring their own food and drinks. Mac would immediately relieve them of their beer, and then, with gracious hospitality, he would offer it back to them during the evening, drinking two of their beers himself to every one he gave to them.

Since he was good with cars, it was Mac's job to work on the jeeps while I took the guests on safari. One day we had more guests than I could take by myself, so we divided them up into two parties, one under me and one under Mac. Because he was new to this, I sent one of our best trackers with him.

While they were on the walk, a thorn bush sprang back at Mac, catching him by his long hair and lifting him partially off the ground. His guests were highly amused that their great white hunter should be hanging helpless in a thorn tree. For once, the easy-going Mac lost his cool completely. 'Cut me loose, you silly bastards!' he shouted. When they carried on laughing, he threatened to load his gun and shoot them. Only then did they free him, which they did by cutting off his long hair.

When we began Londolozi, I had been inspired by our neighbour, Loring Rattray, whose established game lodge, Mala Mala, attracted visitors from all over the world. With a large staff, Mala Mala had something we didn't – girls! There were a couple of unattached receptionists at Mala Mala, so we would drive over at night to see them, taking all our dirty laundry with us. We would park our jeep on a slope and sneak into the staff quarters to get our washing done. We'd also order room service and listen to the Rolling Stones on LP records. When we left, we'd coast down the slope and start the engine when we reached the bottom of the hill. We did this for a few years – management never knew about it.

Whenever there was a party at Mala Mala, which was pretty often, we would go down to join in the fun, and Mac would be the life and soul of the party. No one could match him beer for beer – he outdrank everyone; invariably the rangers would all pass out drunk while Mac was still having the time of his life.

At one party, which was even wilder than usual, with guys passed out all over the place, Mac announced at the top of his voice to whoever was still standing that he was going to do his Flaming A. This involved stripping naked and putting a rolled-up newspaper between his legs, which I would set alight. He would have to run as fast as he could so that the flames wouldn't burn his arse. Unfortunately, due to the amount of beer he'd consumed that night, and because it was dark, Mac didn't notice a drum and a pile of new thatching grass (we discovered later that Mala Mala had just begun thatching the chalets in its new luxury camp).

Moving at high speed with the burning newspaper between his legs, Mac ran straight into the drum and fell over, setting the lawn and the thatching grass alight. The fire quickly took hold, fanned by the wind, and headed rapidly towards the newly thatched chalets.

The night watchman and I seemed to be the only sober people there – the rangers were nowhere to be seen. First we grabbed Mac and pulled him out of the fire and then we set about trying to put out the blaze with our jackets. We managed to stop the fire from reaching the new chalets, but the lawn and most of the piles of thatching grass were burnt.

I knew that there was going to be hell to pay.

Once we'd put the fire out, I piled Mac into the jeep, coasted downhill and drove us home, hoping we might get away with it.

No chance. The next day, Adriaan Erasmus, the manager of Mala Mala, arrived with a letter from Loring Rattray addressed to me, which said, 'I am declaring you and that sidekick of yours, who looks like he has been pulled through the bush backwards by a Shangaan, persona non grata at Mala Mala for the rest of your lives.' This was a devastating blow, because it cut us off from the girls and the parties.

Mac read the letter, pulled deeply on his cigarette and declared, 'I'm going to go and see Mr Rattray and eat humble pie.' He was terrified of being cut off from the parties … and all the free beer!

Mac and I went to see Adriaan Erasmus, who was a friend of mine – he would sometimes ask me to help with game drives if they didn't have enough rangers at Mala Mala. We also used to supply Mala Mala with impala skins for tanning. We threw ourselves at his mercy and asked him to intercede on our behalf with Mr Rattray.

I don't know exactly how he did it, but somehow he managed to soften Loring Rattray's heart and persuade him that we weren't bad guys and should be given another chance. I received another letter saying that the lifetime ban had been lifted on condition that we didn't do it again. So Mac and I were allowed back to Mala Mala, always under the strict supervision of the manager.

For the first couple of years of Londolozi's existence, Mac and I slept in a very basic prefabricated hut with no door. For safety we placed a paraffin lantern in the doorway to deter animal intruders. We built a wall inside the outer wall of the hut to provide insulation against the heat. In time a mamba made its home between the wall of the prefab and the wall we'd built – at night we could hear it moving about, catching rats or whatever it ate. Our only other companion was an Alsatian called Tiger, who had come with me from Johannesburg. There was a partition between Mac's bed and mine, and Tiger slept on my bed.

I noticed one day that wasps were making a nest in Mac's blankets, and I said to him, 'You'd better get rid of that nest.'

'Oh, ja,' he replied in his laid-back way, 'I'll get around to it sometime.' A few days later, I was woken during the night by screaming. I switched on my torch and saw Mac jumping around, shouting, 'I've been stung by these fucking wasps!'

A while later, we were woken by another huge commotion. Looking out through the doorway, I could see that a pride of about thirteen lions had caught an impala right against our hut.

We watched for a while, but then Tiger decided he needed to defend us, so he rushed outside, barking at the lions. A lioness spun around and charged at the dog, who in his haste to return to the hut knocked over the lantern in the doorway, plunging us into darkness. All I can remember is a large furry animal landing on top of me. Fearing that the lioness was on top of Tiger, who was pinning me down, and being able to see nothing in the pitch darkness, I pulled as many blankets over my head as possible. I waited for the growl to come, the death rattle, but there was nothing! When I emerged from my cocoon, I was relieved to realise that the lioness had stopped at the doorway and gone back to the kill.

After a moment, I heard a small voice coming from above: 'JV, are you all right?' I struck a match and lit a paraffin lantern, and saw Mac balancing precariously in the rafters of our hut. In the moment when the lioness had charged, he had sprung from his bed into the roof in one leap – an incredibly athletic feat for anyone, let alone a guy who smoked sixty a day!

* * *

Ultimately Mac wasn't suited to the tourist business. He was developing a drinking problem from all the socialising that went along with it. I said to him one day, 'Mac, if you stay in this business, you are going to go down, and I don't want you to do that. Go and do something else. This kind of business is not for you.'

He left Londolozi and joined Helicapture, a bunch of game-capture guys headed up by the late Keith Coppen, another friend of mine. They were the nicest guys you could hope to meet, but this hard-drinking environment also wasn't the best for Mac.

He went to Namibia for a few years and became the best sable-capture guy in the business. Many cattle and sheep farmers, who were battling to survive in the low-rainfall areas of southern Africa, turned to wildlife, hunting and ecotourism. It was here that Mac made his greatest contribution. He took what he had learnt at Londolozi and, together with Keith Coppen and the Helicapture crowd, stocked thousands of head of game into huge areas of South Africa, Zimbabwe and Namibia.

Tragically, in a moment of black despair, Mac took his own life. He didn't like guns, so I was extremely suspicious when I heard that he had killed himself with a gun.

The good companion was gone.

5

The Guests

The people who visit Londolozi are an integral part of the reserve, not only for the money they bring, but for the energy that they provide. Imagine a soccer match between Manchester United and Liverpool without a single spectator: the crowd at a soccer match is what the guests are to Londolozi.

A beautiful lady who came to Londolozi in the late seventies was the rock-and-roll singer Tina Turner. Tina was relatively unknown in South Africa at that stage. She had been brought out by the impresario Ronnie Quibell as she attempted to resurrect her career after the much-publicised break-up with her husband, Ike Turner. South Africa was still racially segregated in those days, and she was performing in small venues in Johannesburg. She came to Londolozi with her road manager, Rhonda Graam, for some R&R. Strange as it may seem, I had no idea who she was when we first met. I happened to be on the plane that was taking them to Londolozi, and asked them where they were going. Tina was quite shy at first and let Rhonda do most of the talking.

'Where are you guys from?' I asked.

After a few stunned moments, Rhonda said, 'Don't you know who that is?'

'No,' I replied.

'That's Tina Turner.'

'Well, who is Tina Turner?'

'You don't know who Tina Turner is?' she asked in astonishment.

'No,' I responded, 'I have no idea.'

I started chatting to Rhonda, and I don't think Tina liked that Rhonda was getting more attention than she was ... especially when she found out that I was the owner of Londolozi. So Tina and I started chatting.

As we got to know each other during her time at Londolozi, she opened up to me. She told me about her childhood, how she had grown up in a small town in Tennessee called Nutbush, where as a barefoot kid she had picked cotton in the fields. She told me how she'd been a big fan of Ike Turner's when she was a young girl, and how she had gone to watch him play so often that she'd known the words to all his songs. One night his back-up singer hadn't turned up for a gig and she'd begged to be allowed to go on stage with him. That was how she got her first break. She joined up with Ike and gradually became the dominant force in the famous Ike and Tina Turner duo.

After she had endured years of physical and emotional abuse at Ike's hands, Tina's world had come crashing down, and she had literally run, penniless, for her life. When I met her she was in a bad space, still hurting from the abuse and the break-up, and terrified of guns.

One of the things that Tina had turned to for salvation during this dark time was Buddhism. Wherever she went, she took her shrine and she would chant. Rather like a verbal meditation, Tina's chanting gave her enormous power and energy.

My family, on my mother's side, was quite religious, some of them being missionaries who had wandered across Africa spreading the word of God. My father's side was atheist; they were complete non-believers. As a kid, my mother had sent me to Sunday School, but they asked me to leave, so I guess I fell into the atheist category.

Tina showed me how Buddhism was connected to the natural world, and I became quite interested. Today, whenever I have to fill in a form that asks my religion, I always put Buddhist, though, truth be told, today I still know very little about Buddhism. I do regard the bush as my church and tell people proudly that I go to church every day.

Tina taught me to sing and dance and, together with her stage dancers, we had a lot of fun. There are very few camp-fire singers in the world who can claim to have had Tina Turner as their private singing and dancing coach!

In return, I played the fool with her and teased her. I hope I taught her to laugh at herself a little in the process. She had been abused and I was very gentle with her, but I lectured her about taking herself too seriously. I don't think she'd ever met a man like me before. We were from completely different worlds.

Tina reciprocated my hospitality and invited me to go on tour with her. In Los Angeles, she took me to a very famous psychic who had predicted to Robert Kennedy that he'd be killed. Normally you'd have to wait six months to see her, but Tina got an appointment immediately.

So Tina said to her, 'I want you to do a reading on my friend here.'

The psychic said, 'No problem. Tina, get out of the room.' Tina didn't like that – she wanted to know what the psychic had to say. She tried to object, but still she was sent out.

The psychic said to me, 'You will work with an animal that runs with a rocking motion, and there are hundreds and thousands of them! It's a beautiful scene. They are crossing the rivers, and you will go there.' (A few years later I went to Kenya, where I filmed hundreds of thousands of wildebeest crossing the Mara River on their annual migration.) The psychic also predicted that I would work with 'the endangered big cats'. A lot of what she said to me came to pass, but all that Tina really wanted to know was whether the two of us were going to hook up and stay together.

The life of a rock-and-roll singer is completely back to front. Tina would go on stage around 10 p.m. She would play until after midnight and then go for dinner, and she would finally go to bed around three in the morning, getting up at noon the following day.

I quickly realised that this life was not for me. It was not a world in which I felt comfortable. Tina was going to Australia to shoot *Mad Max Beyond Thunderdome*. She invited me to go along, but I contracted malaria and couldn't go with her.

Tina and I wrote a song together called 'Just Another Friend', which she presented to her manager, Roger Davies. Roger is an Australian, and he and I had talked a lot about cricket, which he missed because he lived and worked in the USA. Roger's response to Tina's idea that she record 'Just Another Friend' was, 'JV, I dig you a whole lot, mate, but the anti-apartheid demonstrators are

Me, aged twelve,
with tracker
Winnis Mathebula
and the male lion
I had just shot

Me, aged fourteen, with
the male leopard I
hunted with tracker
Two Tone Sithole

Boyd Varty, my father, hunting on
his beloved bushveld farm, Sparta,
which later became Londolozi

With my mother, Maidie, at my brother, Dave,
and Shanny's wedding – the only time I have worn a tie in my life

An elephant cow tries to lift its young calf after it has been darted in the Kruger National Park in a translocation operation

A cheetah with sarcoptic mange at Londolozi

Darting a mange-infected cheetah with antibiotics to prolong its life

The Mother Leopard, whose life I documented on film for over twelve years, allowed us to follow, film and observe her, giving us privileged access to the secret world of a female leopard

Trying to save a giraffe bull that had slipped at Taylor's Crossing, Londolozi

Tracker and friend Elmon Mhlongo with a poached rhino at Londolozi

A rhino horn – worth more per ounce than gold

Tina Turner during her trip to Londolozi in the late seventies, meeting a young elephant that had been introduced to the reserve

Tina: friend, mentor, teacher and Buddhist

Fleetwood Mac and Cheryl Tiegs, who visited Londolozi in the eighties

Cheryl Tiegs at Londolozi to co-host 'Operation Elephant Airlift' for the ABC television network

Former Miss World Pamella Bordes visited Londolozi in the eighties and was followed by the paparazzi

Brooke Shields playing the part of American documentary producer in the 1992 feature film *Running Wild*, which was shot at Londolozi and in Kenya

Brooke and me on the set of *Running Wild*, where she coached Elmon and me on the dos and don'ts of acting

Preparing the leopards Little Boy and Little Girl for a flight to Kenya during the filming of *Running Wild*

Little Boy in the film *Running Wild*. Since its inception, Londolozi Productions has made over forty films in fourteen different countries

Little Girl on the set of *Running Wild* in the Masai Mara National Park, Kenya

When Gill joined me, she divided her time between 'designer' Johannesburg, where she was South Africa's favourite TV presenter, and the bush, where the living was rough, rustic and unpredictable

A magnificent – and rare – wild king cheetah at Londolozi

With king cheetah Nkosi and normal cheetah Lozi, who were relocated to Tswalu Kalahari Game Reserve

Half-Tail the Leopard in the Masai Mara (left) and killing a gazelle

Filming the wildebeest migration in the Masai Mara, Kenya

A male lion strolls past migrating zebra in the Masai Mara

A female cheetah moves her cub from a burnt area, Masai Mara

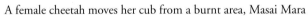

outside Tina's concerts, and now the press has heard that she has a white South African boyfriend. Can't you just hit the road, mate, and go to the Amazon or visit the Eskimos or go somewhere far away?'

I took Roger's advice and, with my 'song-writing career' in tatters, left for an extended stay with the Inuit in Alaska.

Tina's star rose rapidly, and she went on to win eight Grammy awards.

Tina taught me strength; she showed me that when things look desperate and hopeless you shouldn't give up. If you dig deep and persevere, you can still realise your dreams.

Later in my life, when I started the tiger project, I would need all of Tina's inspiration to survive a personal crisis of enormous proportions.

* * *

Another famous guest who visited Londolozi was the comic genius Spike Milligan. The word 'genius' is often bandied about lightly, but Spike was the closest to a true genius I've ever met. He reminded me of an eccentric professor I had at university, who was quite brilliant but often forgot where the lecture room was or what time the lecture was. Spike had a deep concern for the natural world and a genuine interest in all things great and small. He was extremely concerned about what we humans were doing to our environment, so much so that he would become deeply depressed about the state of the world.

He had heard about Londolozi and came to visit for the first time around 1980. The next time he came, he brought his wife, Shelagh, and two of his daughters. He and I had discussions about a wide variety of subjects, ranging from elephant culling and the social system of wild dogs to rhinos and ants. One day while we were on a walk through the bush, I realised that Spike was no longer behind me. After backtracking for several hundred metres, I found him intently studying a colony of ants through his magnifying glass. After observing them for close on an hour, he declared, 'These bastards have a lot more discipline than the British army.'

Spike had a fast mind and a quick wit, and he would often have people in stitches, but he also suffered from bouts of depression. You were never sure which Spike you were going to see on any given day, the happy one or the sad one.

He told me that he could hear infrasound, and during the war he would hear the bombers coming long before anyone else did. So when the other soldiers saw Spike running, they knew they had to dive for cover. One time, while he was staying at my house, he got up, in his pyjamas, and walked to the camp, which is about 300 metres away, where he turned off a fridge because he could hear its low humming. On the way back, he saw a leopard, so he just sat down in the path and meditated with the leopard! The next morning he was over the moon, because he had seen this leopard in the moonlight.

One evening we were sitting around chatting after supper. Spike was quite shy and Shelagh started telling us one of his stories, but she was telling it so badly that he took over. He told me that he had turned down an invitation to Prince Charles's wedding to Lady Diana on principle, to protest against the bearskin helmets worn by the guards. When he was interviewed about this, he said he had worked out that fifteen bears would be killed to make the bearskin helmets that the guards would be wearing.

In the eighties, when I was in London, Spike invited me to meet him outside the Canadian High Commission. When I arrived, he was surrounded by a large crowd and two or three television cameras. Spike was clubbing a dummy seal with an ice pick as a protest against the clubbing of seals by the Canadian government.

The moment he saw me, he told the crowd, 'This is John Varty, a conservationist from South Africa. He'll tell you all about seal clubbing.' And Spike thrust the ice pick into my hand and shouted, 'Hit the seal, man, hit the seal!' I don't think I have ever felt so ridiculous in my entire life, ice pick in hand, whacking a dummy seal on the pavement in London!

Then the interviewer turned the microphone on me. 'What kinds of seals do they have in South Africa?' he asked.

I'd never ever seen a seal but I took a guess. 'Fur seals,' I replied.

'And does the South African government club seals?' the interviewer enquired.

This was the moment Spike had been waiting for. 'Of course they do!' he bellowed. 'They even club people, those apartheid barbarians.'

Spike was determined to introduce me to Peter Sellers, describing him as 'filthy rich and we can get a lot money from him for conservation'. We were to meet Sellers at a restaurant in London, but between the two of them they got the restaurants wrong. The second night they arranged to meet, they got the restaurants right but the time wrong. I never did meet Peter Sellers.

Spike was all action: he put his money (actually, other people's money) where his mouth was. When I first met him, Londolozi had just a few elephant bulls roaming around. He decided we needed more elephants, so he raised £15 000 by persuading many famous people, such as the Beatles, Elton John, the Bee Gees and Peter Sellers, to help us buy elephants. We used the money to buy our first breeding herds of elephant from the Kruger National Park. When Spike came back to Londolozi with his daughters and saw a herd of elephants, he was absolutely delighted. Whenever I see a large herd of elephants at Londolozi, I think of Spike.

* * *

The rock-and-roll group Blood, Sweat and Tears had a hilarious trip to Londolozi some time around 1981. The band had played a concert as a fundraiser to help us buy elephants and were now flying in two aeroplanes (one aeroplane was not enough because the band had collected so many groupies) to Londolozi.

Desperate to show them elephants, I had decided to take them straight from the runway to view four big elephant bulls that were moving slowly towards the Mala Mala boundary. If the elephants crossed the boundary the band would not see them, so I had to move quickly.

The band together with the groupies totalled sixteen people. In their purple hats, yellow T-shirts and polka-dot trousers, the band members looked exactly like what they were: a rock-and-roll group in the bush, absolutely impossible to hide.

The elephant bulls were moving through thick bush, and the Land Rovers could go no further. We would have to continue on foot if we wanted pictures of the elephants. I implored the band to move quietly, to talk in whispers and to follow in single file behind my tracker, Elmon, and me. We moved down a path and into a perfect position in front of a large bull elephant, who was ambling towards us. As the elephant came out into a small clearing in front of us, I noticed, as did everyone else, that his thirty-kilogram penis was hanging down (elephant bulls will often do this to cool themselves).

One of the groupies shouted out, 'Holy shit, do you see that? I must get a picture!' With that, the elephant bull spun around and mock-charged the group. You have never seen sixteen people move so fast and in so many different directions. There was no such thing as ladies first – some of the groupies were trampled underfoot by the band. It took Elmon and me an hour to find the various members of the group. One was hiding in a warthog burrow, one was up a tree and another was in a water hole (he had heard that elephants couldn't swim).

On our return to the runway, the manager of the band announced that nothing could surpass that experience and that he was flying back to Joburg because his drugs had run out. Half of the band of Blood, Sweat and Tears returned to Joburg with him, having never even seen the Londolozi camp.

* * *

On a trip to the United States around 1981, I had met with John Wilcox, a producer at ABC Sports. John was mildly interested in my story about an elephant translocation from the Kruger National Park to Londolozi, when I said, 'John, we are going to airlift the elephants!'

'You're going to do what? Did I hear you say you're going to airlift the elephants? We'll do it!' he exclaimed immediately.

John chose trans-Atlantic balloonist Ben Abruzzo to host the show. I warned John that Londolozi was not good balloon country as every second tree is a thorn tree. Undeterred, Ben and his balloon came along on Operation Elephant Airlift.

My worst fears were realised when Ben took off on his maiden test flight. Within half an hour, he was beyond the boundaries of Londolozi and flying over the Kruger National Park. When finally we were able to make radio contact with him, all he could tell us was that he was in the bush, and that his balloon was wrapped around a thorn tree. I was concerned that perhaps Ben had landed in Mozambique, where there was a war going on. I could imagine the headlines: 'Ben Abruzzo, well-known balloonist, arrested for invading Mozambique in balloon'. In desperation we hired a helicopter, and twenty-four hours later we found Ben, none the worse for his ordeal, in the Kruger National Park. The balloon, however, was a write-off!

Cheryl Tiegs was one of the top models in the United States in the 1970s and 1980s. In addition to modelling, Cheryl narrated *The American Sportsman*. John Wilcox brought Cheryl along to co-host Operation Elephant Airlift. How and why Ben Abruzzo and Cheryl Tiegs ever got to host an elephant show remains a mystery to me to this day. This was entertainment, however, not conservation, and we had a lot of fun making the show.

Cheryl was even more beautiful in real life than she was in her photographs. She was great company and entered into the spirit of the crazy movie that we made. I must say, it was hard to concentrate on the elephant capture when Cheryl was around!

Cheryl's boyfriend at the time was Peter Beard, the well-known and controversial wildlife photographer. Peter had made a career out of photographing wild animals and beautiful women, so he and I had a lot in common and we became good friends.

The capture of the elephants was pretty traumatic. The animals were shot with tranquillising darts from a helicopter. I watched in dismay as a mother and an aunt stood shoulder to shoulder to keep their darted calf on its feet as the drug took effect. The mother did something I had never seen before: reaching down into her stomach with her trunk, she extracted water, which she blew into the face of the drunken calf in an attempt to revive it. When the calf fell, the mother would not leave it but stayed by its side trying to lift it, despite being buzzed frequently by the helicopter. Another distraught mother in the group, using a tall knob-thorn tree, tried to smash the helicopter out of the air as it hovered over the calf.

Elephants are very social animals and it is accepted today that separating young elephants from their mothers will result in problems in later life. Just as human children that have been abandoned or abused at an early age will often become delinquents or turn to crime, so too will elephants. Excessive aggression towards tourist cars, rhinos and other mammals has been recorded in elephants that were separated from their herd when they were very young.

Our knowledge of and sensitivity to elephants was limited in those days of the late seventies and early eighties, and I hope that the stress and trauma created in these early captures will never again be repeated.

As the elephant numbers have grown in the Londolozi area, however, a number of local landowners are again advocating the capture and culling of elephants. When questioned about this, they always give personal answers: 'The elephants are eating my paw-paw trees in my camp.' 'The elephants have ripped up my water pipes.' 'Elephants are killing all the trees in my park.'

Elephants are part of a cycle that changes the habitat. This change is not necessarily bad. They destroy trees but they also create trees by passing seeds through their digestive system. Many of these habitat cycles take longer than a human lifetime. Few of us can comprehend the ecological role elephants play in the natural system.

To counter the ill-conceived plan to capture and cull elephants in the Sabi Sand area, I recently wrote the following newsletter to those in my database:

I see that the Minister of Environment of South Africa has lifted the moratorium on culling of elephant.

Like most people, I admire elephant greatly, although I know very little about them. In my pursuit of cats and while building Londolozi, I have had some unique and rare experiences with elephants that I would like to share with you.

In Kenya's Tsavo West National Park, with the late Bill Woodley, the warden of the park, I had the privilege of flying over a herd of 1500 elephants.

Indeed, as Woodley buzzed the herd in his small plane, the dust was so thick from the fleeing herd that Woodley was forced to take the plane up higher to safety. The scene is still vividly imprinted in my memory.

Bill Woodley told me that 1500 elephants were congregated together, which meant they were being heavily poached. He explained to me that while Tsavo had once been a thick

Commiphora woodland (when they first arrived, they had to cut their way into Tsavo), now it was an open grassland.

The destruction of trees by the elephants had caused Tsavo to become more of an open grassland. The water table had lifted and fountains had begun to flow. Animals that thrived in grasslands had increased. There were many advantages to the change. In short, Bill Woodley had had the rare privilege of seeing a natural cycle of nature moving from woodland to grassland, somewhat speeded up by the big numbers of elephants, in the space of his lifetime.

Scientists had claimed that the black rhino was lost to Tsavo because of the habitat destruction caused by the elephants. They argued that the elephants should have been culled before this was allowed to happen.

Bill Woodley refuted this; he said the black rhino disappeared due to poachers, not habitat destruction. He conceded that the opening of the bush assisted the poachers in locating the rhino. Finally, nature took her own course and large numbers of elephants died in the drought.

In contrast to the Tsavo example, I had the opportunity of observing the intense management system of the Kruger National Park employed during the 1970s and 1980s.

Londolozi is situated in the Sabi Sand Private Game Reserve, which lies on the south-western side of the Kruger National Park. Sabi Sand is a small reserve of approximately 55 000 hectares. When we started Londolozi in 1973, the Sabi Sand had only five elephant bulls. In the Sabi Sand was a veterinary wire fence, which divided the Kruger Park from the private game reserves. This restricted the natural movement of elephant herds.

The situation was ironic. At Londolozi, we were clearing the bush with bulldozers to create open grasslands to try to save grazer species like blue wildebeest, and next door in the Kruger Park, they were culling elephants, an animal that could naturally create grasslands as they had done in Tsavo.

We did two things. Firstly, we campaigned heavily for the removal of the veterinary fence so that the elephants could move freely between the Kruger National Park and Londolozi. This was achieved in the nineties due to the vision of the then Chief Executive Officer of National Parks, Dr Robbie Robinson. In the early eighties we purchased 60 elephants from the Kruger National Park and translocated them to Londolozi.

The operation was a success and the Sabi Sand had for the first time breeding herds of elephant.

Today, with the fence gone and the elephants increasing, in excess of a thousand elephants can be seen in the Sabi Sand/ Londolozi area, mostly in the dry season. Every elephant expert and scientist has an opinion on what should be done. I don't pretend to have any answers, but I make the following observations.

Under the elephant management policy during the eighties and nineties, the Kruger National Park maintained their elephants at around 7 000. Every year the surplus was culled. This was after intense aerial counts were done to determine the numbers.

The Kruger Park was divided into sections and a certain number were culled from each section. Often the section ranger, with the assistance of the ground crew, did the culling, which involved shooting the elephants with a dart loaded with a chemical called scoline. This caused the respiratory system in the injected elephant to stop functioning and death occurred within a few minutes. The culling was conducted over nine months of the year (the cooler months) by highly trained individuals with the best state-of-the-art equipment at their disposal. The size of the Kruger allowed them to cull elephants far away from tourist camps and roads.

The helicopter pilots employed by the Kruger Park were air-force trained and the finest in the land. Literally hundreds of hours were flown without a serious accident.

As the culling operation moved into a section, the area was heavily impacted by helicopters, trucks, front-end loaders and people. Then the operation moved on to the next section, giving the elephants respite until the next year when the culling operation returned.

It's important to understand that a culling operation is not the same as a captive operation. Once an elephant is dead, the carcass has to be butchered. Meat, skin and ivory all have to be preserved. The Kruger Park built an abattoir to accommodate the culled elephants.

Live caught elephants are very different. Each elephant needs its own crate. Despite what they say, larger elephants are more difficult to handle. For this reason, large cows are often cut away and the smaller elephants are captured. This means traumatised cows are left behind and traumatised young elephants are separated from their mothers.

Fewer elephants can be caught than can be culled and therefore, to remove elephants, more captures and more impact will result.

While anyone would prefer capture to culling, the outcome could be very different.

The executive committee of the Sabi Sand (55 000 hectares) have decided to catch 500 elephants and donate them to neighbouring African countries.

I applaud the creative thinking, even though some of the African countries involved do not have a good track record in protecting their elephants.

However, Sabi Sand is relatively small. It has numerous tourist camps in close proximity to each other. At any one time, more than 60 open Land Rovers, each with overseas tourists in them, are criss-crossing the land. Many of these people are wealthy high-profile people. The Sabi Sand does not have the luxury of the vast open sections of land found in the Kruger Park. Indeed, one section in the Kruger may be bigger than the entire Sabi Sand.

More than 30 capture operations in Sabi Sand will have to be carried out by the private enterprise to catch 500 elephants. They have neither the expertise nor the equipment or the safety record that the Kruger National Park has.

The private enterprise is profit driven; they will not have the luxury of operating at a steady pace like the Kruger Park could do, moving from section to section. The helicopter pilots are commercial, often flying many hours a month. They have no-where near the experience of the Kruger Park's original pilots.

Helicopters are by their very nature dangerous machines and the private enterprise's track record for accidents is high.

But it is perhaps the trust between man and elephant that will quickly be totally destroyed.

I worked in Kenya's Masai Mara for 17 years and filmed many elephants with wire snares on their trunks and feet. I saw enraged elephants attack and kill Masai herdsmen.

I filmed in Zambia's Luangwa Valley for 14 years. Luangwa once supported 100 000 elephants. At Shingalana Camp, few elephants if any had any tusks at all. The elephants with tusks had been poached.

One day I was chased by a tuskless female for two kilometres before I found a suitable tree to climb. I vividly remember the hatred in the elephant cow's eyes as she circled the tree trying to get me.

Helicopter pilots in the Kruger National Park told stories of how cow elephants had lured the helicopter down and then tried to smash the helicopter using a tree. Another cow, who had lost her calf, had got her trunk onto the skid of the helicopter and had tried to pull it out of the sky.

These are highly intelligent animals, using everything they can to ensure their survival against the technological advantages at the disposal of human beings. Understandably, they have extreme hatred for human beings.

It is more than 25 years after we first introduced breeding herds of elephant into Londolozi, and today, you can sit quietly in an open Land Rover and cow elephants with young calves will graze and browse within a few feet of you.

A unique partnership with the world's largest mammal has been formed and it has taken a long time.

It goes something like this:

I have land and plenty of bush to share with you. I have built many large dams for you to drink from and to swim in.

I have removed the wire snares that can injure you. I have not hunted you for trophies. I have not captured you and separated you from your family.

You have responded with trust. You have not smashed up aeroplanes worth millions of rands standing on the runway. You have not attacked the people in open Land Rovers and turned the Land Rovers over.

This unique partnership of trust is in for a rude awakening, and the human beings who implement this decision to capture 500 elephants in a small area called Sabi Sand are in for a bigger awakening. It could be a disaster for humans and elephants.

Ironically, after 25 years of increasing elephants, I am still using a bulldozer to clear the bush to try to save the grazers. In short, the elephants have not done it for me.

Like Tsavo, rivers at Londolozi have begun to flow where elephants have killed trees in the catchments.

Yes, marula trees and knob thorns have been killed by elephants at Londolozi and, yes, many young marulas and knob thorns are surviving and thriving. Many of these have germinated in elephant dung.

The only constant in life is change and, yes, the elephants are changing the habitat. Like the Tsavo situation, that change can sometimes be for the better.

My letter had the desired effect, and the capture and culling have been halted.

* * *

One night in the late eighties, I returned late to camp after filming in the bush. The Londolozi rangers informed me that Pamella Bordes was in camp. 'Who is Pamella Bordes?' I asked. The beautiful Indian-born Pamella Singh had won the Miss World contest in 1982, and Bordes was her married name.

When I met her, she told me that she was a wildlife photographer and asked if she could come filming with me. Normally I film alone. Perhaps it was because of the smell of her perfume, or her impressive photographic equipment, or some obscure pheromone, but after some persuasion I agreed that she come filming with me the next morning.

It soon became apparent that Pamella was not alone at Londolozi. The following day, some paparazzi flew in, having come all the way from England, intent on getting pictures of her in the bush. Pamella, who seemed really frightened, asked me if she could hang out at my house to avoid the paparazzi. Not to be outdone, the paparazzi hired their own jeep and went on game drives, trying to trace us through the two-way radio, hoping to get pictures of Pamella and me filming in the bush. Soon she became too scared to come on game drives with me, and begged to be allowed to stay at my house instead.

The reporters asked if they could come to my house to do an interview with her, but she refused point blank to let them anywhere near her.

While we were on our game drives, she told me her story. She said that she had recently caused havoc in the Thatcher government because she had simultaneously been involved with several senior newspaper reporters and the Minister of Defence. Confidential security secrets had appeared in the newspapers and the media had tracked the source back to Pamella. Overnight Pamella became a target for the British paparazzi.

She told me how the paparazzi had pursued her when she was riding on a motorbike on Bali, causing her to have a serious accident. They had laughed and taken pictures of her lying bloodied and injured in the street, without offering her any assistance.

When Princess Diana subsequently died in the tragic car accident, it reminded me strongly of Pamella's story. It is clear to me that hyenas have more ethics than some of the photographers who pursue celebrities.

I realised that, if we were to get rid of the parasitic paparazzi, I would have to lead them on a wild-goose chase, so I organised for a pilot friend of mine to mention to them that he was flying Pamella and me to a game lodge in Namibia.

The paparazzi immediately chartered an aeroplane and were last seen flying out to Namibia. Pamella and I flew to Kenya to photograph Kilimanjaro before going to Zimbabwe to canoe down the Zambezi River.

After Pamella returned to England, pictures appeared in the *Sun* newspaper, accompanied by an article in which Pamella called me a sex machine and said that, during our safari, she and I had used more than a gross (144) of condoms. This would have averaged out at more than four condoms a day. A reporter from the *Sun* phoned me up and asked if this was indeed true. 'No, it's not true. It's a gross underestimation!' I replied.

* * *

The well-known actress Brooke Shields arrived at Londolozi in 1991 to act in *Running Wild*, a feature film about the life of the

Mother Leopard, which starred Little Boy and Little Girl leopard. Brooke played the part of an American documentary producer. Elmon and I appeared in the film too, and Brooke was great fun on set as she coached us on the dos and don'ts of acting, something we knew nothing about.

In our documentary film making, we were used to having only one chance at a shot rather than as many as twenty takes, which is what often happens in feature films. Brooke was happy to share from her experience as an actress to help these two rookies.

For Elmon and me, who were used to working as a two-man crew, to be involved with a crew of thirty or forty people was quite intimidating. What we found really hard to accept was that the crew stuck firmly to their union rules. One day while we were following the Mother Leopard – who was a celebrity in her own right – the crew stopped for lunch, despite my protests, and the Mother Leopard disappeared into the bush. We missed a great shot. Elmon and I had never seen anything like it.

The movie, directed by Duncan McLachlan, with big names Martin Sheen, David Keith and Brooke Shields, did extremely well at the box office. It had some strong conservation elements in it and I enjoyed being a part of it. For me, however, a feature film is about entertainment, whereas a documentary is about educating through reality.

Ultimately, my personality and Elmon's weren't suited to feature films. After *Running Wild*, we were more than happy to go back to our two-man crew to make more documentaries.

* * *

Perhaps the most famous guest ever to visit Londolozi was Nelson Mandela. He first came shortly after he was released from prison, in 1990, with Enos Mabuza, leader of the former KaNgwane homeland, and Thabo Mbeki, who went on to become the second democratically elected president of South Africa in 1999.

Dave and I had many conversations with the three of them on the verandah of my house, discussing an idea we had to privatise the Kruger National Park. The concept revolved around allowing private enterprises to enjoy tourist concessions inside the park. Mr Mabuza had already implemented this practice in his own homeland. In the course of one of these conversations, I said to Madiba, 'Mr Mandela, you know that the grasslands of South Africa's Karoo used to support more wild animals than any country in the world?'

He said, 'What do you mean?'

'There used to be a hundred million springbok or more,' I replied. 'There were so many animals that wagons were stopped. In fact, one year they overran Beaufort West and flattened the town.'

'You know, in prison, somebody gave me a book and I read about that,' he responded. 'I sat in my cell and I imagined these vast herds of animals.'

'You know, you can get it back,' I said to him.

He was curious to know what I meant, so I explained my thoughts: 'Well, there are hundreds of farms in the Karoo. These farms are mostly owned by Afrikaners. The land is given over to sheep, which are exotic to Africa.' I told him how sheep destroyed the land by overgrazing it.

He said to me, 'Oh, John, but we could never take the land

away from the people. That would not be in line with the policy of the ANC.'

'A vast part of South Africa is being turned into a desert by this land-use system,' I replied. 'The sheep-farming system is flawed, and the people running it are destroying the land.'

'So are you telling me that we are destroying the natural resources of South Africa with the system?' he asked. 'That is another matter.'

Years later, when Thabo Mbeki was president and I had already started the tiger project, a delegation of four men arrived to speak to me. They said, 'President Mbeki sends his regards to you and wants to remind you of the talk you had at your house. We are designing a park that goes right around the Orange River from the town of De Aar. How would you make this park?'

'There is only one way,' I replied. 'You have to buy the farmers out.'

'That is going to cost a lot of money,' they retorted. 'We think we can rather involve the farmers in the park.'

'No, I have already tried that and it doesn't work,' I said. 'You have to buy the farmers out. Compared with what we spend on defence, it's not a lot of money, and you will be able to get the Serengeti of the south back. Plus, it will bring thousands of tourists into the area and create jobs. Here at Londolozi, I employ 209 people and I feed a thousand people. You need to make the National Parks Board and the private enterprises sponsor schools and clinics, to uplift the people.'

They loved that idea.

A few years later, when I was doing *Safari Live* for National Geographic, I was on the road to the Kruger. Wherever I looked I saw signs saying, 'This clinic is sponsored by the National Parks

Board' and 'This school is sponsored by the National Parks Board'. I was thrilled.

Madiba returned to Londolozi in June 1993 with just a couple of bodyguards. At that time, multiparty negotiations to end apartheid were under way in Johannesburg at the Kempton Park World Trade Centre. I understood that Madiba was deliberately absenting himself for four days, to allow then President FW de Klerk and ANC Secretary General Cyril Ramaphosa to handle the negotiations without him.

During his stay, Madiba told me that he was frustrated with Mangosuthu Buthelezi, the leader of the Inkatha Freedom Party. 'I am not phoning Buthelezi again,' he said. 'I've tried phoning him eleven times and I will not phone again.'

I said to him, 'Mr Mandela, you know something? You are the statesman. You are the only hope of South Africa. If you have to phone Mr Buthelezi twenty times over, that's what you have to do, because you know that the South African government is trying to drive a wedge between you and Buthelezi. It is their aim to turn this into a tribal war between the Xhosa and the Zulu, and it looks as if they are going to achieve it.'

The great man listened to me gravely and, after thinking about what I had said, he said he would take my advice.

Madiba has a great sense of humour. One day while we were on a game drive, I said to him, 'Mr Mandela, I read once that you removed the cockroaches from your cell and set them free, outside. You didn't kill them. Is it true?'

'Yes, it's true,' he replied. 'Just because they locked me up for twenty-seven years, why should the cockroaches have been locked up as well?'

A few days later, we were out on a game drive with Mandela's bodyguards sitting in the back of the jeep. The two-way radio rang out: it was the manager at Londolozi saying that Madiba urgently needed to return to camp. We raced back. When we got to camp, we heard the news that the radical right-wing organisation the Afrikaner Weerstandsbeweging (AWB), which was opposed to the talks, had driven an armoured vehicle into a window of the World Trade Centre, enabling its armed supporters to storm into the building.

Mandela immediately phoned Cyril Ramaphosa, who had sought shelter under a table, and I could hear the shots being fired in the background while they were speaking. I was convinced that this was the start of civil war in South Africa. Mandela was pale and shaking. He was facing a huge crisis in the country's history.

After he had finished speaking to Ramaphosa, he pulled a notebook out of his pocket and handed it to me with trembling hands. 'Get De Klerk on the line now!' he ordered.

I dialled the number that was pencilled faintly into the notebook, and FW de Klerk answered. I handed the receiver to Mandela, who barked, 'De Klerk, I am giving you two hours to control the security forces. If you don't have them under control in that time I am mobilising MK.' MK – Umkhonto we Sizwe – was the armed wing of the ANC.

Mandela had no patience with what De Klerk was trying to say and cut him short with the words, 'You heard what I said. You know what I mean. Get those guys under control now. I will be monitoring it, and if you have not achieved that in two hours, I will put the full force of Umkhonto we Sizwe against you.' And he slammed down the phone.

As I stood alone in the room with Madiba, listening to him on the phone to the then president of South Africa, I had no doubt about where the power lay. Madiba was commanding; De Klerk was obeying.

He turned to me and ordered, 'Get a helicopter to meet me at the airport.'

'Why do you want a helicopter?' I asked.

'Because my people are under attack. I must be with them!' he replied.

And I said, 'Mr Mandela, that is not what I would do. That is a big mistake.' (In this way, I take after my father: I am always getting into trouble for speaking my mind without being invited to.)

He turned to me and screamed, 'Don't tell me what to do! I must be with my people. They are under attack. It's a battle. It's a war, and I am the leader of the people.'

'If you fly to the World Trade Centre, some AWB radical will shoot you,' I ventured. 'You'll be dead, and South Africa will be plunged into a civil war. All that you've fought for will be lost! I'm a white South African and I will be nowhere.'

'Don't tell me what to do. Just do what I tell you!' Madiba shouted, and he stormed out of the room.

I began to organise his helicopter. Mandela was sitting in the next room with his hands clasped as if in prayer, deep in thought. There was nobody else around. After twenty minutes he came back and said, 'So, John, what do you suggest?'

'Mr Mandela,' I said to him, 'I suggest that when you land in Johannesburg, you go to your house. I will organise for the SABC [South African Broadcasting Corporation] to meet you there. Go on television and address the nation. Tell them that these guys who've attacked the World Trade Centre are a small minority group that don't represent the South African public. Tell everyone to remain calm. That is my advice to you.'

He looked at me, and he thought for a moment, then he said, 'Cancel the helicopter. I will do as you say.'

I drove him to his plane, and he shook hands with me and said, 'Thank you. You have given me good advice at a difficult time.' And he walked away.

Two hours later, we switched on the TV and there was Madiba calming the nation, explaining the situation and leading South Africa into less turbulent waters.

It is a mark of Madiba's greatness that he was able to stop and take advice from a younger white man in such a time of crisis. I believe that his greatest strengths are that he is such a good listener and that he is able to understand other people's cultures and speak to people on their terms. It was a quirk of fate that I, a man who knew nothing about politics (I don't read newspapers or watch television, and I had no idea before Mandela arrived that these peace talks were even taking place), was with Nelson Mandela at Londolozi at such a crucial moment in South Africa's history, when he should have been surrounded by the leaders of the ANC.

Without Nelson Mandela's great leadership, South Africa could have been a very different place from what it is today. I had experienced a defining moment in the history of the country. It was indeed an honour and a privilege to witness the great man in action in one of the gravest moments of our past.

When Madiba later spoke at the Ezemvelo KwaZulu-Natal Wildlife centenary celebration, he said in his address that he dreamed of a time when all South Africans, black and white, would be working for the good of conservation, just as we were doing at Londolozi.

After his address, my brother, Dave, who was attending the celebration, went up to him and said, 'Mr Mandela, thank you for those kind words and for mentioning Londolozi.'

Madiba said, 'And, tell me, where is John?'

'He is in Zambia,' Dave replied.

Without hesitating, Madiba said, 'Tell him the liberation struggle is over. He can come home now!'

6

The Tracker

As a young boy I spent many days hunting with the great Harry Kirkman, much of whose time was devoted to trying to catch poachers. Over the years, I have come to realise that it is an exercise in futility. Wherever you have poor communities living alongside wild animals, you will have poaching.

During night patrols, Harry would tell me of the most famous poacher of all, Engine Mhlongo. Engine was the poacher Harry most wanted to catch, but Engine could run like the wind and none of Harry's game scouts could match his speed.

Engine operated alone, unlike most other poachers, who worked in gangs. He wore shoes he had made from old tyres, with the track of the shoe pointing backwards to deceive the game scouts. Many hours were wasted following his tracks before the game scouts discovered that they had been tracking Engine in the wrong direction.

Engine hunted using bows and poisoned arrows so that he could kill a buck in absolute silence. His camps were extremely well hidden in the bush – no one could find them.

When we started Londolozi in 1973, we decided to follow a

different route from the norm. Many of the poachers lived in the former homeland of Gazankulu, which borders Londolozi. Some of them had well-deserved reputations as fearless hunters and brilliant trackers. Our rationale was that, if we could offer them a job tracking lions and leopards for our guests, they would be earning cash and would not need to poach.

One name that often came up among the poachers as a brilliant tracker and a man of incredible bush craft was Elmon Mhlongo. Never having been to school, Elmon had no formal education – he couldn't even write his name – yet he could read a track the same way I could read a book. When asked if there was any animal he couldn't track, he answered, 'Only a bird.'

I asked him one day who had taught him to track, and he replied that it had been his uncle, Engine Mhlongo. Elmon told me that Engine had been a master tracker, a great hunter, a loner and a mystery man. Elmon had been a runner for Engine: he would often meet him in the bush and take the meat of the game Engine had caught to the local villages to sell it.

Elmon said to me that Engine had been a living legend among the local Shangaan people because of his bush craft. They believed that he didn't run away but disappeared into thin air – he had the mystique of a witch doctor about him. His independent lifestyle inspired great admiration among the locals.

When he was older and couldn't run as fast as he had been able to in the past, he was finally caught. Elated that he had at last apprehended Engine, Harry Kirkman sent three of his best game scouts to escort him in handcuffs to the magistrate's office at Bushbuckridge. The party camped on a small river near a village, and all the villagers came out to see Engine because he was such a celebrity ... it was as if Michael Jackson or Elvis Presley had arrived in town. Out of earshot of the game scouts, he told some of the village women to bring lots of strong marula beer for the scouts. When Engine spoke, you did what he said – he had that kind of presence – so the women rushed off to get the beer.

The game scouts were in a jubilant mood, having captured their high-profile prisoner, so they happily accepted the beer. By midnight, the three of them had passed out drunk. Engine told the women who had brought the beer to rob the drunken game scouts and bring him the keys for his handcuffs.

After freeing himself, he handcuffed the game scouts to a tree and threw the keys in the river. When they woke up in the morning, not only did they find themselves attached to a tree, but their prize trophy was gone.

Harry Kirkman never managed to catch Engine again.

Elmon, like his famous uncle, believes that ownership of wild animals is a white man's concept. Cattle, sheep and goats can be owned, but wild animals belong to everyone. Therefore, when Elmon hunts an impala or snares a duiker, he believes he is only taking what is rightfully his.

When I began working with Elmon, I soon realised that he regards the bush as a giant pantry. You just need to know where to look, what to catch and how to find it.

Over time I hired many poachers and turned them into successful trackers. I admired their skill and knowledge of the bush. One of the things I most enjoyed was going out for a day tracking leopard with a group of trackers. They are fun to be with and have lived free and uncomplicated lives.

In 1984 I decided to make a film that would show the fascinating lifestyle of a hunter. The role of the hunter was played by Elmon Mhlongo. During *The Crossover*, Elmon's character taught mine the tricks of survival.

The public's reaction to the film was interesting to say the least. White people hated it and black people loved it. It was obvious that the whites thought we had glamourised the life of a poacher. It was unacceptable for a poacher, whom many whites regarded as an uneducated savage, to be teaching an 'educated' white boy; they couldn't see that poachers had any place in conservation.

The point that I was trying to make in *The Crossover* was that knowledge does not just come from books, schools and universities. Poachers, or hunter-gatherers as I prefer to call them, have a wealth of knowledge that has never been written down. People who live off the land have a practical, hands-on approach to life. The Masai in Kenya, with whom I developed a close bond over the course of seventeen years, also have this kind of knowledge, which no amount of book-learning can teach.

Elmon knows an enormous amount about the natural world, such as which plants are safe to eat and what you can use to poison fish and then still eat them. As the old trackers die, that knowledge is in danger of being lost: the modern Shangaans go to school, where they receive a Western education, and none of them live off the land the way their fathers have done.

The Crossover was filmed in 1984, the height of apartheid in South Africa. The country's national and provincial parks were there for the pleasure of the white people only. Indeed, if you were a black person and you wanted to visit a park for recreation, you couldn't do so. At most, you could stay in a separate, second-class camp.

The white establishment believed that poachers were the scourge of the park system. They were to be caught and punished – sent to jail or even shot dead if necessary. Ignorant savages had no place in the white man's conservation ethic.

When a senior National Parks official heard that I had hired poachers to become trackers, he said bluntly to me, 'They will slit your throat and then steal your game!'

Our experience at Londolozi has been that poachers make the best game rangers. Tourists who come to Londolozi all want to see leopards, and who better to find them than a skilled tracker who knows how to read the bush? At Londolozi we have many fine trackers – some of the best in Africa. They have taken the skills they learnt as hunter-gatherers and applied them to modern tourism. Their tracking experience makes them excellent at finding animals for our guests.

Elmon told me the story of poachers from a different perspective. Poaching is time-consuming and dangerous, he explained, and most of the time it ends in failure. They would catch an impala in a wire snare, and then, evading the game scouts, they would return to their snares, only to find that the hyenas had stolen the meat.

On one occasion Elmon had caught a wildebeest in a snare. The vultures saw the dead wildebeest from the air and began to drop. This attracted the game scouts, who took the meat to sell it themselves before resetting the wire snares. In other words, the game scouts were in competition with the poachers. They drew a salary as game scouts, but could make more money by selling the meat of the animals caught in the poachers' snares. All the game scouts had to do was to get to the snared animals before the poachers.

But, occasionally, the high risks that poachers took were rewarded. Elmon told me that a fellow poacher had once caught a sub-adult wildebeest in a snare. As the noose tightened, the animal gave off a distress call. The call was heard by a nearby leopard, which moved in to catch the trapped wildebeest. The leopard then got caught in a second snare (poachers will often set a line of snares). Later, a lioness, reacting to the sound of the suffocating wildebeest, moved in and got caught in a third snare.

When the poacher arrived at the scene, the wildebeest, the leopard and the lion were all dead. He sold everything – the meat, the skins, the teeth, the claws, the bones, the whiskers and the fat – making more money from this catch than a game scout's salary for an entire year.

While white people reacted negatively to the film *The Crossover*, black people appreciated the fact that a white guy would even be interested in how a poacher lived. They also liked that the film didn't portray them as savages, but showed their culture and their bush craft favourably. One old Shangaan man said he liked *The Crossover*, but couldn't I at least have given Elmon a shirt to wear during the film?

In the mid-eighties I made a documentary called *The Silent Hunter*, which followed the life of the first habituated leopard at Londolozi, the Mother Leopard. Elmon and I had spent many hours trying to find her. Often we would leave our jeep and track her on foot, which could take several hours. On locating her, we would return to our jeep and then approach slowly in the vehicle, which acts as a mobile hide, moving closer and closer. It was a painstaking process, but as we persevered she gradually allowed us to approach in the vehicle. Eventually Elmon and I were able to film her.

Elmon has travelled with me to more than ten countries making wildlife movies. To travel, Elmon needed a passport. Since he was not sure of when he was born, I invented a date, making him roughly the same age as me.

In 1983 Warren Samuels, a Kenyan ranger who had worked at Londolozi, suggested I come to Kenya to film the spectacular wildlife and especially the great annual wildebeest migration. During those bad apartheid days, South Africans were banned from many countries, including Kenya.

I obtained Paraguayan passports for Elmon and myself, as these were acceptable to the Kenyan authorities. The customs officials checked the passports of people who were flying in from what was then Jan Smuts Airport in Johannesburg, but they didn't check those of people arriving on planes coming from Mbabane. So for nine years, to avoid suspicion, we flew on Swazi Air in to Kenya and then drove to our tented camp in the Masai Mara.

One day, as we were going through the Kenyan border, a customs official became suspicious. As far as he knew, there were no black people in Paraguay, so he went to call his supervisor. Elmon and I had just come from filming jaguar in the Amazon, and I had learnt some Spanish words. In desperation, I said to Elmon, 'Whatever I say, you just say "*Sí*".'

When the supervisor arrived I launched into a combination of gibberish and the odd Spanish word. Every time I paused, Elmon said '*Sí*'. Apparently satisfied that we were fluent in Spanish and were indeed Paraguayan, the supervisor stamped our passports and we were through.

On another occasion, when we were passing through Jomo Kenyatta Airport in Nairobi with film cameras, it appeared that one of the reference numbers on a camera of ours was wrong. The customs officer informed me that it was a big problem, and that the only way the problem could be solved was for me to pay him a bribe of $15. When I said that I had only a $20 note on me, he replied with a big smile that that was no problem, he had change.

I was keen to make a film featuring three spotted cats, and went on my own into Manú National Park, an extremely remote park in the Peruvian Amazon, to do reconnaissance. I decided while there to include the rare and elusive jaguar in the film. I asked Elmon to join me and bring all my cameras and plenty of film with him. He had to catch three connecting flights to get himself and the cameras to me in Peru, which was a tough ask for someone who was not used to airports, was not fluent in English and didn't know how to read or write.

Elmon arrived safely in Peru with the cameras, but the film had gone missing in transit. We searched all over Lima for two days until we found an old retired cameraman who used to work for the BBC. He had eight rolls of film in his fridge, which he sold to us. The film was about three years old, but we weren't in a position to be fussy. From there we took a light aircraft to the Amazon, where we landed in the middle of the jungle.

Elmon's tracking skills turned out not to be very effective in the jungle, which was much denser than the terrain he was used to. We realised that our only hope of finding the jaguar was by taking a boat and looking for it on sandbanks.

Through our Spanish-speaking guide and interpreter, the local Machiguenga people shared their extensive knowledge of the jungle with us. They led us to another tribe, who took us hunting, but they made us leave the cameras behind – we weren't allowed to film anything. They showed us how they hunted howler monkeys with bows and arrows, and they allowed us to try out their hunting equipment.

Elmon is interested in anyone who lives off the land, and he was fascinated that the locals shot fish with their arrows, while he either catches it with a line or poisons it.

It was an enthralling trip. We saw giant otters and unfamiliar trees and birds. We encountered two naked local women who had been separated from their tribe, and we took them in our boat to the game warden. Finally, after about eight weeks in the jungle, we found the jaguar and got our shots.

The film we made, *Swift and Silent*, won American Cable TV's ACE Award in Los Angles in 1992, beating 200 other films, among them BBC and National Geographic documentaries. The film was shot off the hip and made entirely without a script, budget or shot list. This was guerrilla film making at its best.

One year we were in the Masai Mara illegally filming the wildebeest migration over the Mara River. The area was zoned off because there had been several fatal attacks on tourists by the aggressive Wakuria people, who had crossed over from Tanzania. The attacks had been so severe that the Kenyan army had moved in.

Although my Masai partners tried to dissuade me from going to the crossing point (the Masai are particularly scared of the Wakuria because they have access to automatic weapons), I was determined to capture the wildebeest crossing the river.

After filming through the morning, Lakakin, my Masai partner, insisted we leave the area to return to camp. When our jeep
broke down, the Masai abandoned us and Elmon and I were left
in the danger zone with the broken vehicle.

Mechanically I am more than useless, but, cool as anything,
Elmon went under the bonnet and worked his way through all
the possible problem areas – coil, points, distributor, carburettor,
fuel lines – until he found the fault. He had never had any formal
mechanical training, but he is always watching and learning from
people – he had watched mechanics fixing cars and had taught
himself the basics that way.

During that same trip, Elmon, Warren Samuels and I captured
the now-famous sequence of seventeen gazelles being caught by
the crocodiles as the herd of twenty-two tried to cross the Mara
River. This sequence remains one of the most dramatic crocodile
predations ever caught on film.

Elmon belongs to the old school of trackers. Through his filming and tracking work, he has been able to give his children a
good education. All of them have received a Western education;
none of them will have the bush skills that Elmon possesses.

The Bushmen, the Native Americans, the Inuit, the Australian
Aborigines and the Amazonian Indians, to name just a few, are
without a doubt some of the greatest naturalists the world has
ever known. A common thread runs through these cultures: 'Live
symbiotically off the land, respect her and the creatures with
which you coexist. Tread lightly on her, and she will provide.'

As I write this, the global population approaches seven billion
people. Most of these people live in consumer societies, and all
are burning fossil fuels. Some of the fallout scenarios of global

warming are frightening to say the least. It is certain that Western cultures are not living symbiotically at all with Planet Earth. Our footprint is heavy, and our respect for fellow creatures diminishes as we strive to feed our rising human population.

Many ecologists, biologists and scientists now believe that Planet Earth will move to a new ecological position that ensures the survival of the planet but not necessarily that of seven billion human beings.

Perhaps the survivors will be those who, like Elmon, have developed a symbiotic relationship with our planet.

One of the T-shirts that are sold at Londolozi bears the following quotation, which I hold dear: 'The World is Waiting For a New Direction, One Based on the Laws of Nature'.

7

The Cameraman

He's an artist, he's a poet
He's a scientist, he's a vet
A big cat communicator
An adventurer of note
He's a maverick film maker
And he plays by his own rules
Patience is his password
Action is his cue
  – from the song 'The Cameraman'

I fell into wildlife film making almost by default. I had been escorting guests into the bush for nearly ten years and I was completely burnt out. The personal questions that the guests were always asking drove me mad, so I decided to take a break from tourism.

In the late seventies I met a wealthy, fast-living young film maker from Johannesburg by the name of Rick Lomba. He approached me to use Londolozi as a location to shoot a feature film based on the famous South African novel *Jock of the Bushveld*.

I replied that there were more important things to film, such as how we were destroying wildlife to make way for domestic stock, which in turn was turning the low rainfall areas of Africa into deserts.

Rick became interested, and in 1986 he asked me to be a consultant on a film called *The End of Eden*, which showed the iniquitous veterinary fences in Botswana that were causing the death of thousands of head of migrating wildlife every year, and were paving the way for the huge government cattle schemes that still exist in Botswana today.

Filming with Rick was an interesting experience in itself. His first movie camera was written off in a crash in a microlight. The microlight was being used for aerial photography but failed to take off from a waterlogged strip. Rick smashed the second camera on a tree after he had been bitten by one too many tsetse flies.

My job was to take the finished film *The End of Eden* and, sponsored by the Ford Foundation, do a world lecture tour high-lighting the destruction of the wildlife and the desertification caused by domestic stock in Africa.

The money for the lecture tour never materialised, so Rick gave me his only remaining camera, an old CP16 movie camera, as payment for my work on the film. My curriculum vitae now read: 'Have camera, will travel.'

The inimitable Rick Lomba continued to live life at a fast pace, eventually dying tragically in the jaws of a starving tiger in the Luanda zoo in Angola in 1994. Ironically, in that same year I started my project to save the endangered tiger.

It was with the camera that he gave me, and no training or experience – in fact, very little other than enthusiasm and a strong desire to communicate – that I formed Londolozi Productions. I see film making as a way of telling stories through tools such as a camera.

Londolozi Productions started off as a one-man band, and then Elmon came on board. Over time it grew into a large production company with a staff of around fifteen. We had cameramen in Zambia and Kenya, film editors – the works. Londolozi Productions has made over forty films in fourteen countries and produced some four and a half million feet of film – one of the biggest private wildlife film libraries in the world, if not the biggest.

Today the company has come full circle and is a one-man band once more. Now I make films for other companies, such as Aquavision, National Geographic and the BBC. I present the films and I capture the footage, but the films are made on commission.

The American business tycoon and philanthropist Ted Turner owned a production company called Turner Original Productions that made documentaries. Pat Bennett, a high-ranking member of his team, came to Londolozi a few times and liked our films. She went back to America and spoke to Ted about us, and Turner Original Productions commissioned Londolozi Productions to make a film on leopards called *A Secret Life*.

I went to Atlanta for the final edit and the launch of the film. I met Ted for lunch one day and he told me about this film to which he'd bought the rights, *The End of Eden*, which had greatly influenced his decision to replace domestic stock with American buffalo on his vast ranches in New Mexico and Montana. Proudly, he told me that he owned the biggest herd of buffalo in all of the USA. When I finally managed to get a word in, I told him that I had written the script for the film. Ted stood up from the table, shook my hand and said, 'Thank you for the script. Rick Lomba, rest your soul in peace.'

I like Ted a lot. Although he is very wealthy, he hasn't lost touch with his roots. As a very young man he used to help his father with advertising billboards. There was a long queue outside the restaurant we'd tried to get into that day, a restaurant that he owns. Instead of pulling rank to get us a table, he took us to a real working man's café in an industrial area, where the guys were all wearing overalls. He was totally at ease in that environment. He is a real person and he has done a lot for conservation.

I have never regarded myself as an artistic or classic film maker. My style in those days was to make films from the hip, without a budget or a shot list. I was an opportunistic film maker, and I usually had two or three movies on the go at the same time. One film judge said of my work, 'Varty breaks all the rules,' while another one said, 'Varty doesn't even know the rules.'

My brother, Dave, tried to persuade me to formalise my film making with budgets and deadlines, so we budgeted and planned a film on hyenas. We went to the Masai Mara to shoot it, but there was not a single hyena to be seen: the Masai had poisoned all of them. Instead, we shot a film called *Troubled Waters* that went on to win awards. When you're shooting nature, you can't plan everything the way you can with a feature film that is shot on set with actors.

These days, if you want to make a wildlife film, you have to sell the concept to a broadcaster, then you have to try to make it within the producers' budget and answer to their demands, and usually they know nothing about Africa. It used to be much more fun making films the way we did, where we had far more freedom. It was adventurous and opportunistic, and at times it was dangerous.

I have a desire to communicate what we are doing to this beautiful yet fragile planet and the havoc we are wreaking on rare and sensitive endangered species. We are a voracious species and to feed ourselves we are prepared to push everything aside in the pursuit of what is called progress.

I made a documentary, *Survival on the Savannah*, on the African buffalo for Discovery Channel. Towards the end of the film is my favourite part of all my films, the Gaian section, in which I address the audience with a message from my heart. In *Survival on the Savannah* I informed the audience that we were destroying the buffalo home range and replacing the buffalo with cattle. The cattle would go on to overgraze the land and, in order to keep them going, we would send them to feed lots.

When we were filming the giant feed lots in Texas, I had been appalled by the conditions I saw, and especially by what was being fed to the cattle. Instinctively I knew that this was a recipe for disease and disaster. With no hard facts to back it up, I made the prediction in the Gaian section of the documentary that a catastrophic disease would break out in the feed lots.

Discovery Channel was not impressed. 'Re-edit the film,' I was told. 'You have no hard facts and if this is true, it should come out on the news, not in a buffalo documentary.'

So the Gaian section was edited out and, two weeks after completion of the film, bovine spongiform encephalopathy (mad-cow disease) broke out across Europe, causing millions and millions of dollars' worth of damage.

'Re-edit the film; put the Gaian section back immediately,'

they told me. But it was too late: the film had been released without the Gaian section.

I am always amazed at the power and the reach of documentary films. Some of my documentaries have been screened in as many as 160 countries. Wherever I go in the world I meet people on whom the films we've made have had an impact. A few examples spring to mind.

In the Amazon jungle, a group of American bird watchers recognised Elmon Mhlongo from the film *The Silent Hunter*. I watched as Elmon, in his rather broken English, enthralled his American audience for over an hour with his leopard stories.

In the Negev Desert, two Israeli scientists took me to a rickety research hut. In the hut was a generator, a TV monitor and a faded copy of *The Silent Hunter*. Among their notes were a dozen questions about leopards, which I was happy to answer.

Outside Ranthambore National Park in India, I was waiting in a jeep in the queue for the gates to open. A vendor came to my window and tried to sell me a copy of *Swift and Silent*. Close inspection revealed that it was a pirated copy.

I was driving through South Africa's Great Karoo one night and was running low on fuel. I pulled into a village to fill up. As the pump attendant put diesel in my car, I saw him looking at me in the light of a street lamp. Finally he said, 'Hoe gaan dit met Shingalana?' (How is Shingalana?) After he'd finished filling up my car, he fetched his old video-tape copy of *Shingalana*, which I autographed for him.

On another occasion I was driving through South Africa's Free State province. In the back of the jeep, covered by a tarpaulin, was the adult tigress Julie. A traffic cop pulled me over and began to examine the jeep, which had no licence disk, no roadworthy certificate and no third-party insurance. In fact, it had not been on a public road for fifteen years.

'What's in the back of the jeep?' asked the cop.

'A tiger,' I replied.

'Maak jy grappe met my?'(Are you joking with me?) said the cop.

He lifted the tarpaulin and there was Julie gazing back at him.

He turned to me and said, 'Ek ken jou. Ek het jou op TV gesien. Jy is die tier man.' (I know you. I've seen you on TV. You're the tiger man.)

The cop then called his assistants and took pictures of Julie and me and four traffic cops with his speed camera. After the photo session the cop pulled me to one side. 'You have committed a serious offence,' he said. 'I must confiscate your jeep.'

'What will you do with the tiger?' I asked.

The cop smiled. He hadn't thought of that. He thought for a moment and then he said, 'You know, my children have all your videos but they don't have *Living with Tigers*.' As luck would have it, I had a DVD in the jeep, so I reached inside and gave it to him. His face lit up. 'Now remember, we never had this conversation, understand?'

'Completely,' I replied.

As I drove off, his parting words to me were, 'One day when I have enough money, I want to save tigers and make films like you.'

8

Gill and Shingalana

Living at Londolozi and filming at night I seldom got to see any television, but occasionally I would go to my brother Dave's house to watch the sport or the news. I noticed, as did every South African male at the time, an incredibly beautiful woman reading the news. Her name was Gillian van Houten.

I came up with the idea of writing her a letter. I addressed it 'Gillian van Houten, TV Presenter, SABC'. Before I could post it, I managed to mislay it and had to write another one.

The thrust of the letter was, 'I think you are beautiful but you are wasting your time reading the news; you should be making the news. You should come and make movies with me across Africa.' Talk about a direct approach!

I am not good on paper, and on a previous occasion I had written two letters to two girlfriends and then put the letters in the wrong envelopes, so they reached the wrong ladies. This ended two potential romances quite swiftly.

Both of my letters actually did reach Gill, so she must have known that I was keen to meet her. For reasons I don't begin to understand, she agreed to hook up with me and suggested that we meet in a restaurant in Melville, close to the SABC studios in Johannesburg. I got the wrong restaurant, however, and missed the date completely. Gill suggested that next time I should bring my tracker with me.

She came to Londolozi with friends, spending a few days there. I was about to set off for Kenya for a couple of months. 'I'm going to make a movie in Kenya,' I said to her. 'Do you want to come with me?' I wasn't expecting her to say yes, but for some reason she did. She must have thought it was a risk worth taking. So she gave up her career and joined me while I made movies around Africa – in Londolozi, in the South Luangwa National Park in Zambia and the Masai Mara in Kenya.

Gill was born and bred in the suburbs of Cape Town. Her life at the SABC was structured and organised. She had any number of eligible bachelors vying for her hand. Why she chose to pursue a chaotic, unpredictable lifestyle with an eccentric maverick like me only she can know. One newspaper article encapsulated the situation when it showed a picture of Gill and me with the caption: 'What's South Africa's best-dressed lady doing with South Africa's worst-dressed man?'

During our years together, Gill endured many hardships, including malaria, tsetse flies and helicopter accidents, and finally gun attacks by mercenaries. It is a testament to her tenacity and perseverance that she survived this harsh existence for fifteen years. Gill was close to the lioness Shingalana, Little Boy and Little Girl the leopards, and the tigress Julie, and she has an incredible affinity with big cats.

Gill gave me the three most beautiful children any man could wish to have. Savannah, now fifteen, and the twins, Sean and Tao, ten years old, have transformed my life. Of all the projects I have worked on, the films I have made, the friendships and relationships I've had, and the dangerous encounters I've experienced, nothing remotely matches the joy of having a family and watching the miracle of one's children growing up.

The fact that my relationship with Gill was never formalised with marriage was entirely my fault. I guess my wild lifestyle and the freedom with which I was used to living made me unsuited to a conventional marriage. Gill has proven herself to be an outstanding mother to our children, dedicating herself to their welfare for over fifteen years. She has given them a conventional, grounded upbringing that will stand them in good stead in later life. While I have been a lousy partner to her, I have tried to be a good father, teaching our children the values I learnt from my parents, siblings, family and friends, not to mention the great cats with which I have shared my life.

Many people ask me if my children will follow in my footsteps and do what I do. Of course nobody can answer that question – I thought I would be a professional cricketer and ended up a wildlife communicator. Our children may become sportspeople, actors, writers, television presenters or conservationists. They will choose their own roads and undergo their personal evolutions in the process. All we as parents can do is try to give them sound values, such as honesty, loyalty, good manners, sportsmanship and a sense of fun and adventure. My advice to any kid growing up is that life is a journey; take it with both hands and live it like there is no tomorrow.

If our children take up the challenge of working with cats as both their parents have done, they will experience joy, sadness, disappointment, inspiration, courage, loyalty, intelligence, speed, power, beauty, joy, joy and more joy.

* * *

One morning in the early nineties, the radio sounded at Londo-lozi. Over it I heard the voice of Andrew Lewis, a game ranger who was out on a game drive. 'JV, I have found a single lion cub that has been abandoned.' Elmon, Gill and I raced out to find a tiny lion cub, just hours old, dehydrating in the hot sun.

This cub had been born to a young female in the Sparta pride. It may have been her first litter. She had given birth to the cub and simply walked away. When lions produce a single cub they rarely raise it; it's just not worth it, when four months later they could produce a bigger litter of three or four cubs.

Gill picked up the minute cub and Elmon said, 'Her name is Shingalana' (which means 'small lion' in Shangaan). We didn't know it at the time, but Shingalana would, over the next three years, take us on a journey that would profoundly change our lives. For three years we slept, hunted, filmed, studied and communicated with Shingalana. The experience opened up an entirely new world for us.

It was interesting to observe the different reactions of the three of us to Shingalana. Gill, who had not yet had children, was definitely Shingalana's mother.

Elmon couldn't see the point of giving up a comfortable bed and moving into a tented camp in the bush for the sake of a lion. As a kid, Elmon had competed with lions. They had chased him into trees and stolen his father's goats and cattle. 'She will bite you before Christmas,' Elmon warned.

I saw our relationship with this young lioness as a natural progression in the understanding of big cats. I had spent weeks, months and years studying the Mother Leopard from a jeep. Now that I had the opportunity to learn from a lion at close quarters, I was elated!

Everything I do in the bush is recorded on film. My camera is my diary; I seldom write anything down. Little did I know that day that the film *Shingalana* would turn out to be one of the most exciting, informative, inspiring, profound and ultimately tragic films I would ever make. Shingalana took me to some of the highest points in my life, and when she died I was devastated. I didn't recover for a long time.

Lions are pride animals, and they have a huge capacity to love. Gill, Elmon and I were the only pride Shingalana ever knew.

We set up a tented camp on the edge of the Mashabane River bed. The Mashabane (which means 'river of sand' in Shangaan) is a dry river that passes through the core of Londolozi. Lining its banks are some beautiful trees, including ebonies, figs, marulas, and weeping boer beans. Gill and I stayed with Shingalana at the tented camp while Elmon came out every day with food from the main camp.

For Gill it was a time of great contrasts in her life. She had become South Africa's favourite TV presenter on a show called *Premiere*. Every Thursday she would catch the Comair flight from Londolozi to Joburg and present the show on Friday night. Then on Saturday morning she would fly back to Londolozi to the Shingalana tented camp. At the SABC, she was pampered by make-up artists and hairdressers; at Shingalana Camp she had a basin in the bush for a bath, a drop toilet and paraffin lanterns for lights. Talk about the diversity of life.

For me the camp was ideal. I prefer a tent to a house – the less I have to clean, the better. Time means nothing to me (I have never owned a watch). In the bush, days become weeks, weeks become months, and months become years. In a tent, I'm close to nature, surrounded by an Eden of plants, insects, reptiles, birds and mammals. I was in the middle of Londolozi, one of the most beautiful places on earth.

Shingalana was the focus of my world as I watched, photographed and filmed her journey to adulthood. It was a magical journey of wonder to be with this beautiful, kind and affectionate, yet powerful, creature. It was a rare privilege.

I'd wake up early and take Shingalana hunting down the river bed each day. Often I would take a soccer ball and kick it to her. Lions have forward-facing eyes and, like humans, their judgement is excellent. Their powerful legs can propel their supple bodies into the air with effortless ease. To observe Shingalana chase, leap and catch balls flying through the air was like watching an Olympic athlete. On average, a soccer ball would last four days – Shingalana went through more than two dozen soccer balls in those early months.

One morning, two male lions (one was Shingalana's father) caught a buffalo near Shingalana camp. Being an orphan, Shingalana was ignorant of how to behave around male lions, and she went out to investigate. Next thing she came racing back into camp with a huge male lion chasing after her. She dived into the tent and crawled under the bed, and, luckily for us all, the confused lion returned to his kill.

Taking Shingalana out hunting every day proved to be outstanding training for the young lion. In the process of learning how to hunt, she was bitten by a python and struck by porcupine quills before finally catching a newly born impala fawn, which she brought proudly back to camp.

One night she caught a grey duiker outside the tent. I could hear the distress call of the duiker as Shingalana tried to throttle it. I was not the only one who heard the call: within minutes, three hyenas arrived on the scene. With a paraffin lantern in my hand, I decided to try to help Shingalana defend her kill from the hyenas. The only problem was that I hadn't communicated my intentions to Shingalana, and she, like the hyenas, thought that I was trying to steal her kill. A swift swipe and her dewclaw opened up a nasty gash down my thumb.

The intelligent, opportunistic hyenas watched intently. Realising that the lion and the human being were not exactly working together to defend the kill, the hyenas stood shoulder to shoulder and moved in menacingly.

Standing in the dark with just a paraffin lantern, Shingalana and I were no match for the snarling hyenas. One came from the front, the second bit her on the rump and, as she turned, the third grabbed the duiker in its powerful jaws and ran.

* * *

Londolozi is not an ideal place to release a lioness that has no fear of human beings. There are too many tourist camps in and around the Londolozi area into which Shingalana could casually have strolled, scaring the life out of the tourists. I couldn't take that risk.

When she was one year old we decided to move Shingalana to a remote part of the South Luangwa National Park in Zambia. With heavy hearts, we immobilised the young lioness and flew her to Mfuwe, the headquarters of South Luangwa.

Waiting at the airstrip were several hundred Zambians, mostly women and children. In the Nyanja culture, if a woman can get her child to touch a live lion, the child, they believe, will have courage for the rest of its life.

After literally hundreds of small hands and feet had touched the unconscious Shingalana, we loaded her into the Bell JetRanger helicopter. Rob Parsons, the pilot, and Dewald Keet, the vet, flew sixty kilometres down the Luangwa River with Shingalana and me, to the remote camp site I had chosen.

My camp consisted of nothing more than one tent for both Shingalana and me. When we landed, Shingalana was still unconscious from the drug. As it was getting late, Rob and Dewald set off immediately so that they could land in the last light back at Mfuwe. As the helicopter disappeared from sight, I realised I had no light, no torch and no matches to make a fire. It was just me and an unconscious Shingalana in a dark tent.

Things went okay until about midnight, when Shingalana began to wake up. The drug used to immobilise a lion can cause it to become very aggressive when it regains consciousness. I thought Shingalana would recognise my voice, but it had no calming effect on her whatsoever. Reality suddenly dawned on me: I was confined in a small tent, at night, with no light and a powerful, aggressive lioness who showed no sign of recognising me. I decided to abandon the tent and climb into a tree outside. There was no moon and it was exceedingly dark.

Inside the tent, Shingalana was on her feet but still very groggy. As she fell against the tent poles, she growled. Our situation was dangerous to say the least. I was in a medium-sized tree with a drunk, aggressive, growling lioness trapped inside the tent below me. I had no light and poor night vision on a dark night. My biggest fear was that Shingalana's growling would attract wild lions, who would see me as an easy meal and attack Shingalana. The only weapon I had to defend us with was a .44 Smith & Wesson revolver.

Eventually the tent split open. Shingalana fell outside in a dazed state and wandered off into the darkness.

I have never been so happy to see the sunrise as I was after that interminable night. When I climbed down from the tree, Shingalana was nearby and still very uncoordinated.

Because of the long journey from Londolozi to South Luangwa and then the helicopter flight to the camp, Shingalana had been unconscious for a total of sixteen hours. This is a long time to keep a lion anaesthetised and the heavy dose of drugs had no doubt caused the aggressiveness the night before, as well as her inability to recognise my voice. As I sat next to her talking softly, she gradually began to recognise me and eventually made a full recovery.

Our routine in Luangwa was pretty much the same as it had been at Londolozi, only now we weren't hunting in a dry river bed; we were hunting along a big river with an estimated 30 000 hippo and fourteen crocodiles per mile.

All that remained of the once-large elephant herds in the park were tuskless females (the poachers had spared them, as they possessed no ivory). These females were the most dangerous elephants I had ever encountered anywhere in Africa.

While I was out hunting with Shingalana one day, a tuskless female elephant picked up my scent and, from nowhere, she charged. I turned and ran, trying desperately to find a suitable tree to climb. After being chased for more than a kilometre, I eventually spotted a tree with low enough branches for me to clamber into. For over an hour, the elephant cow circled the tree, her eyes blazing.

I wondered what pain she must have experienced in her life. How many of her family had she seen brutally killed at the hands of poachers that she had such a hatred for human beings?

Finally the cow, realising that she couldn't get to me, ambled off. It was another hour before I found the courage to return to the ground and continue hunting with Shingalana.

In the dry season, the massive hippo population of Luangwa is placed under enormous pressure when it comes to grazing and water. Sometimes several hundred hippos crowd into shallow pools as the Luangwa River ceases to flow. It is during this time that fighting breaks out among the hippos.

One morning Shingalana and I came across two hippo bulls fighting ferociously, their mouths agape. Hippos have enormous canines and if one bull can flick the other onto its side, he will use these canines to stab the opponent, often with fatal results.

Shingalana and I watched the bulls fighting. I was getting some excellent footage when, to my dismay, Shingalana decided to play a game of Chase the Hippo. One of the bulls, deciding that a lioness combined with another hippo bull was too much to handle, turned and ran for the opposite bank. As he crossed the shallow water, I noticed that he was bleeding on his rump and flanks. Hotly pursued by Shingalana, he ran for cover into the dense riverine thicket.

Camera in hand, I followed the wounded hippo bull and Shingalana ... a most unwise thing to do. The visibility was less than three metres, and thorns and creepers retarded my progress.

Foolishly I followed the blood and spoor of the wounded hippo. Suddenly there was an almighty roar, and Shingalana came running straight towards me ... with an enraged hippo bull hot on her heels.

I turned and ran, but I knew that there was no way I could outrun the hippo, which was already moving at high speed. The thorns tore at my clothes, the vines entangled me and the hippo came crashing straight through it all like a tank. And then suddenly, there was silence ... nothing!

Thankful to be alive, and in a state of shock, I continued on my way and didn't go back to see what had happened to the hippo. The following morning, while Shingalana and I were out hunting, we found the hippo bull lying dead below the bank of the Luangwa River.

On examining the tracks carefully, I realised what had happened. As we had fled from the hippo, Shingalana and I had, by a stroke of luck, run close to the river bank. The winding Luangwa River floods in the summer months, and the force of the water undermines the banks, leaving them susceptible to collapse. Under the weight of the hippo (bulls can weigh three tons), the bank had caved in, sending this massive bull crashing fifteen metres to its death into the river bed below. Mother Nature had smiled kindly upon us at a critical moment.

Shingalana soon attracted the attention of the local lions. One lioness, who appeared to be a loner and was not part of a pride, would come to call. Shingalana would join the lioness and for two or three hours they would be out hunting.

I was hopeful that the two lionesses would join up, come into oestrus together, mate with male lions and give birth to cubs, forming their own small pride. Unfortunately it was not to be. Shingalana was too bonded to her human pride and would always come back to us. (Conversely, Little Boy and Little Girl, the leopards that had featured in the movie *Running Wild* with Brooke Shields, were released very successfully in Luangwa in Zambia; because there were two of them, they were less bonded to humans than solitary Shingalana.)

At three years of age she came into oestrus, and this immediately attracted the attention of the territorial males. Unfortunately, the wild lionesses were in oestrus at the same time (it is well documented that lionesses' oestrus will synchronise so that they mate and produce cubs at the same time) and competition for the males was intense.

On one incredible night I was having dinner with Gill, Elmon and a film assistant named Karin Slater, who had joined Shingalana and me. Shingalana was thirty metres away from us, and two beautiful dominant males were lying ten metres from her. Later, as one of the males tried to mate with Shingalana, the lionesses arrived and all hell broke loose.

The lionesses, intent on killing Shingalana, lost all fear of us human beings and, although we fired shots over their heads to try to scare them off, we had little initial success. Led by a large lioness called Mangy Face, the lionesses attacked again and again. It was chaos, with lions running through the camp and Shingalana diving into tents for safety.

Whether the wild lionesses knew instinctively that Shingalana was a nomadic lioness, whether they resented the competition for their pride males, or whether they perhaps regarded her association with human beings as inappropriate, I don't know. What I do know is that Mangy Face and her pride spent a lot of time and energy trying to kill Shingalana, until they finally gave up and left.

Because of the danger, we tried to walk Shingalana with two people at all times. One day, when Elmon had malaria, I went out on my own with the young lioness. We crossed the river where it was fairly shallow and started moving upstream, looking for puku or impala to hunt. Suddenly, Mangy Face and four other females emerged from the bush, moving menacingly towards us. When Shingalana saw them, she immediately ran behind me and submitted on the ground. Mangy Face came to within twenty metres of me and also crouched on the ground, growling threateningly. My .44 revolver had five rounds in the cylinder (if Elmon had been with me, we would have had the .375 with us as well). I fired the first shot into the ground in front of Mangy Face, trying to spray the sand into her face. She retreated about ten metres, still facing us and growling threateningly.

I walked backwards, Shingalana right at my heels. Mangy Face came forwards at a crouched run, and I fired a second shot that stopped her but didn't force her back. Mangy Face was now about ten metres away from us, intent on getting to Shingalana. Again we tried to back up, and again the lioness made a short charge. I fired more shots but they were having less and less of an effect.

At this stage, things became blurred in my mind. I knew that I had started with five rounds in the revolver and I had fired four of them. My strategy was that, if Mangy Face crossed an imaginary line I had drawn in the sand, I would be forced to shoot to kill with my last bullet.

I could see the lioness summing up the situation. If she could kill the puny human being, then she would be able to get to Shingalana and she and the other four lionesses could easily kill her.

Suddenly Mangy Face charged me. Confident that I had one more round in my revolver, I waited until she was close, aimed between the eyes, and fired. The revolver went 'click'. Instantly I realised with horror that I was out of ammo. From that moment things seemed to unfold in slow motion. Shingalana met the charge full on. I fell over and, as I recovered myself, Shingalana and Mangy Face were rolling over and over in the sand, fighting viciously.

I was in the classic fight-or-flight state. The river was twenty metres behind me. I could turn, run and swim across the river, leaving Shingalana to her fate, or I could enter the fray and help Shingalana.

Apart from my revolver and my camera, both of which were useless protective tools, I carried with me a metre-long sjambok (a large whip made from hippo hide). Slashing left and right, and using every foul word I could think of, I entered into the fray. Mangy Face, finding herself up against both a lioness and a human being, took fright and retreated about thirty metres. This was my opportunity – running backwards, Shingalana and I made for the river.

I dropped the revolver and the camera and entered the river as silently as I could. The water was deep for about seventy metres, so I swam under the water, trying to make as little disturbance on the surface as possible, as this would attract the crocodiles. Shingalana swam next to me above the water.

Luckily it was ten o'clock in the morning, when most of the

crocs would be basking in the sun and not very active, and Shingalana and I made it across to the other bank. I noticed that, although it was a hot day, Shingalana was shivering. Then I too began to shiver. In fact, both of us were going into a state of shock. For more than an hour, lioness and human being sat together, comforting one another. Both of us knew that this traumatic experience had been a close call. There was no doubt that Shingalana, by meeting the charge full on, had saved my life, and, equally, there was no doubt that, by entering the fight, I had saved hers. I had probably used up at least one of my nine lives that morning.

Some time later, I came down with a bad dose of malaria. Luangwa is renowned for its malaria, especially the feared cerebral malaria that is often fatal. Malaria is a dangerous disease if not treated properly, and I have lost several friends to cerebral malaria. My policy when anyone got this disease was to fly them to South Africa, where there are good medical facilities.

Gill was back in South Africa, so I instructed Elmon to barricade my tent with thorn bushes so that Shingalana could not get in – she had got into the habit of sleeping with me in the tent.

During the night I tossed and turned, sweating profusely, the tent spinning as I hallucinated. My temperature was climbing and I was afraid that the illness could turn cerebral.

Around midnight, the top of the tent split open and in came Shingalana. Obviously concerned for my well-being, she immediately began to lick my sweaty face. A lion's tongue is covered in tiny sharp barbs – it was like being rubbed with sandpaper. I was too weak to get her off me and was barely able to shout to Elmon for help. When Elmon heard my feeble cries and tried to remove Shingalana from my tent, she was having none of it. Eventually

I had to put a pillow slip over my head to protect my face from her rough tongue.

In the morning, I was unable to walk, and Elmon, Lloyd Gumede and John Knowles carried me across the sand to the boat. (Lloyd is a Shangaan man who came with me from Londolozi to help with filming in Luangwa, and John, a former Londolozi ranger, was now one of my film assistants.) Shingalana stayed with me every step of the way and, after they had laid me in the boat, she plunged into the river, swimming strongly next to the rubber duck for a distance of some 300 metres.

On reaching the opposite bank, Elmon, Lloyd and John laid me on a mattress and we began the three-hour journey to Mfuwe to catch the plane.

The trip was an interminable nightmare, as I had to stop several times to vomit. I was barely conscious when we finally arrived at the Mfuwe airport, but I could hear the jet taxiing out. 'JV, we have missed the plane. It's taking off,' said John.

'John, stop the plane. Whatever you do, stop the plane, and tell them it's life or death,' I pleaded.

Through hazy eyes I watched John walk out in front of the jet, blocking its path so that it couldn't take off. The pilot shouted for him to get out of the way.

'JV's dying. You've got to take him to Lusaka,' John shouted to the pilot.

'Okay, bring him,' called the pilot.

John, Lloyd and Elmon loaded me like a sack of corn into the plane. The aircraft was full, so I lay in the back on top of the baggage, thankful to have made the flight.

The air steward then arrived and demanded that I get off the plane because I didn't have a ticket. When I refused, he began to try to force me off. With all my strength, which by this stage was not very much, I clung to a seat.

Several passengers came to my aid, holding me by the arms while the air steward tried to wrestle me by my feet out of the door of the aircraft. I managed a few weak kicks at his head.

Finally the pilot intervened. 'Can't you see he's dying from malaria?'

'He's not dying; he's got a kick like a mule. If I let him fly without a ticket, I'll lose my job,' retorted the air steward.

'And if I don't fly, I'll lose my life,' I replied.

Eventually the pilot told the air steward not to be an idiot and to let me fly.

When I arrived, I discovered that Gill was also down with malaria and already in hospital. From our hospital beds, Gill and I watched on television the miracle unfolding as Nelson Mandela was sworn in as the first black president of South Africa. South Africa had taken its first steps to becoming a true democratic country.

After two weeks, I had recovered from the malaria and flew back to Mfuwe. I tried to radio from Mfuwe to Shingalana Camp to let them know that I was on my way, but the radio was out of order. When I arrived on the opposite bank of the river, to my surprise, Shingalana was waiting for me. The greeting she gave me is something I'll remember to my dying day. For more than an hour she jumped and rolled on me, licking my face. For the rest of the day, she didn't leave my side. It was the most touching greeting and the most wonderful display of affection I have ever experienced in my life ... from a human or an animal.

Lions are the only social cats of the big cats, and their capacity to love members of their pride is enormous. That day, I felt what a privilege it is to be greeted by such an emotional, loving, beautiful lioness.

Later, Elmon told me that Shingalana had waited for me every day on the bank of the river and then, on the day I came back, she had crossed the river. Some telepathic instinct had told her that I was returning that day, and she had swum across the river to wait for me.

Several weeks later, I had to return to South Africa to begin the edit of the film we were making on Shingalana. Elmon called me from the crackling radio telephone at Mfuwe. I could barely make out his voice at the other end of the line, but the gist of what he was saying was that Shingalana had been in a fight with Mangy Face and was badly hurt.

I immediately flew to Lusaka and met with a vet, who gave me antibiotics, antiseptic and syringes. The vet offered to fly with me to Shingalana Camp, but I declined the offer. I said we would speak on the radio and I would monitor Shingalana's progress. This was the first of two terrible mistakes I would make.

When I reached Shingalana, I found that she'd been badly mauled, probably by more than one lion. There were claw marks on her back legs and a deep bite near her spine. On her stomach was a single deep wound where a canine had penetrated. I immediately set about cleansing the wounds and giving her antibiotics.

Gradually Shingalana's superficial wounds began to heal, and I thought she was improving. One morning, however, she began to decline rapidly. In desperation I tried to get her onto a drip. It was no use. She died in my arms at midday.

The second mistake I had made was thinking that because the wounds were healing she was going to be all right, when in fact a secondary infection had set in in the deep wound in her stomach. Had I brought the professional vet with me, I might have been able to save Shingalana's life.

Shingalana's death was a devastating blow and it took me several months to recover, during which time I didn't pick up a camera or do any of the things I normally do. The mistakes I had made haunted me for years, and even today I find it difficult to come to terms with her death.

Losing her was like losing a human member of my family. I realise that Gill, Elmon and I managed to give her three beautiful years. These remain three of the most wonderful years of my life. Shingalana taught me a great deal about lions and about life itself, and she undoubtedly saved my life when she met Mangy Face's charge head on. Shingalana gave the word 'love' a new meaning for me. From her I learnt the extent to which lions are bonded within a pride and how exuberantly they express their love for each other.

I have tried to encourage my children to touch, hug and embrace each other and their parents as often as possible, whether they are children or adults. It is a physical expression of affection that I was taught by Shingalana.

At Londolozi there is a dam called Shingalana Dam. It is a place where Shingalana often used to go: it is there that she took her first steps to becoming a fully fledged hunter, and it is there that she was chased by her first rhino.

Often I will sit at the dam alone and feel Shingalana's presence deeply. The rub of her head, her lithe, smooth body against me, her rough tongue licking my face, her incredible love. It is doubtful that I will ever again in this lifetime experience the love I felt for and from Shingalana.

Lakakin wears the lion-mane headdress, which can be worn only by warriors who have killed a lion single-handedly with a spear

With Lakakin Sukuli, a Masai partner of mine, at a Masai ceremony

Gill being painted for a Masai ceremony

Lakakin's second wife on her wedding day

Consulting a Masai Laiboni, a local witch doctor

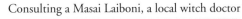

Gill milking a cow belonging to the Masai

With my Masai partners at a Masai ceremony in Kenya. For the seventeen years
that I filmed the annual wildebeest migrations on their land
in the Masai Mara National Park, we were partners

Gill and Savannah at a Masai ceremony where
Savannah was given the name 'Nashipai', meaning 'the happy one'

The orphaned lion cub Shingalana took us on a journey that would profoundly change our lives: for three years we slept, hunted, filmed, studied and communicated with her. From top: Shingalana, three weeks old, receives fortified milk; Shingalana at seven weeks of age; Gill with a growing Shingalana

Gill playing soccer with Shingalana at Londolozi

Shingalana punctured more than twenty soccer balls

Shingalana relaxing with Gill:
Shingi slept in our bed

Gill and Dr Dewald Keet helping to move Shingalana to Zambia.
On arrival, she was to turn aggressive as a result of the tranquillisers

With Shingalana at sunset on the banks of the Luangwa River, Zambia

A hard day at the office

Gill, Shingalana and me at the Luangwa River

The Luangwa River, Zambia: wild, volatile and unpredictable

Gill, Savannah, Mama Hilda and me in a 'banana boat' on the Luangwa River

My office in Luangwa

Our camp on Leopard Island burnt down after Little Boy the leopard bit a gas pipe

Jamu, the 'leopard orchid', whose mother was killed in a poacher's snare

Gill, Jamu and me on Zebra Plain, Zambia, where we filmed Jamu's journey as she was reintroduced to the wilds

Jamu playing with Ngulia the warthog at Tundwe Camp on the banks of the Luangwa River

From top: Jamu as a cub with toilet paper on top of our tent;
Jamu playing ball; an older Jamu on the banks of the Luangwa River

9

Eagle in the Sky

The South Luangwa National Park in Zambia is one of the great parks in Africa. Over the course of fourteen years I spent three months each year making films and reintroducing cats into the wild in Luangwa. Three times I came close to losing my life there, yet time and again Luangwa draws me back like a magnet.

Perhaps it is the thousands of hippo and crocs of the great Luangwa River. Maybe it's the big unpredictable river itself, the feeling of a vast wilderness or the friendly people. I'm not sure, but one thing I do know: I will always return to Luangwa.

* * *

The year is 1995 and I am in Luangwa to shoot *Survival on the Savannah*. I am flying with Rob Parsons, the brilliant helicopter pilot whom I call Eagle in the Sky. It is early morning and we are flying in a Bell JetRanger helicopter over the Luangwa River. A large herd of buffalo is moving down to the river to drink. Rob manoeuvres the chopper over the herd and I turn the camera to 100 frames per second. The light is perfect and I roll some incredible shots of the herd stampeding through the river.

That afternoon I ask Rob to find the same herd of buffalo and put me down in front of them. The idea is that he will drive the herd towards me with the chopper so I can get shots that will cut with the aerial shots captured that morning.

Into the back of the helicopter climb Elmon Mhlongo, Willie Sibuya, an elderly tracker from Londolozi, and Karin Slater. I am sitting in the front with Rob.

Conditions are perfect as we fly along the Luangwa River about 400 feet above the ground, looking for the buffalo. We are some seven kilometres from the camp, when suddenly there is a loud crack and the helicopter lurches sickeningly forwards.

Rob shouts to me over the radio, 'I think we've been shot at by poachers.' We had been doing a lot of anti-poaching work the week before, so this is a reasonable guess.

He can tell from the way the chopper is spinning that the tail rotor has gone. We are spinning out of control. Rob is a veteran of the Rhodesian war, with 11 000 hours in helicopters. Now he is facing the biggest challenge of his life – to get a damaged helicopter onto the ground without killing himself and his passengers. It is every helicopter pilot's nightmare.

'What's it like on your side?' he yells at me. 'Can I bring her down there?'

'No! You can't land here!' I shout back. 'There is nothing but big trees and thick riverine forest. You have to try to swing inland.'

The five people trapped in the helicopter react totally differently from each other to our shared imminent fate as the aircraft begins to fall, like a stone.

Rob is flicking a series of buttons, turning off the fuel switch so that we don't burst into flames on impact. He is desperately trying to control an uncontrollable helicopter. He has turned the engine off and is doing an autorotation – harnessing the energy that is left in the blades to land – so that we will crash in an upright position. When a helicopter's engine fails, an autorotation is a relatively simple manoeuvre to do, but, without the tail rotor, it is practically impossible.

If the chopper rolls over when we land, we will all be killed.

I am looking at the ground below for a place to crash. 'Move away from the river,' I scream. 'Aim for that space between those mopani trees.'

Karin is reciting an Indian mantra to calm herself and relax her body for the impact.

Elmon has decided he is going to jump from the falling chopper. He undoes his seat belt and steps onto the skid. He is planning to jump as we approach the ground and then roll clear of the helicopter. His only problem is that the ground is covered in sharp mopani stumps that could impale him as he lands.

Willie wraps his arms around Elmon, trapping him in the helicopter with the words, 'Hi ta efa hi Makokwana' (We must die together with Makokwana – this is the name the Shangaans have given me as I have got older, describing how I walk with bended arms).

Rob gets us a little way inland to a spot where there are two mopani trees spaced about three metres apart. At the top of the trees he loses all control. If we hit one of the trees, we will fall to our deaths. Gravity pulls us down and we plummet towards the ground, nose first. With a sickening bang we land, and I feel a terrible impact on my back.

As we hit the ground all I can think is that I must get clear of the helicopter, as it could explode at any second. I loosen my safety belt but I simply can't lift myself to get out of the chopper – there is something radically wrong with my spine. I am not in any pain, but my back is numb.

Luckily, the helicopter has split open on my side and I am able to roll myself out, head first, onto the ground. I try to walk a few steps to get clear of the shattered helicopter, but my body just isn't cooperating.

Rob is even worse off than I am. There is something wrong with his back too, and, in addition, he has a broken ankle. The impact of the crash has pushed him down into the cockpit, crushing his chest. He can't free himself and is battling to breathe.

Because the helicopter crashed nose down, the injuries of the guys at the back seem to be less severe. Elmon and Willie cannot walk but they manage to crawl a few metres clear of the stricken helicopter. In a deep state of shock, they aren't able to offer any advice on how we can get out of our predicament. Elmon is usually brilliant in a crisis, but he is too shocked and in too much pain to be of any help. Willie can't speak; he just lies on the ground, groaning.

Our one hope of getting out of this situation lies with Karin, who, mercifully, is able to walk. She is injured and dazed and confused, but she is the only one of our party on her feet. She has to go for help.

Karin has lost her sense of direction and says to me, 'Where is the camp?'

'Walk to the river,' I reply. 'When you reach it, you must turn right so that you are heading west and you will come to the camp. This isn't the shortest route, but you won't get lost that way. Rob, do you have the coordinates so the search party can find us in the dark?'

Rob reads the coordinates of the crash site to Karin through the shattered windscreen, and she writes them down on a piece of paper with a pen she has found in my bag.

'Help me to my feet,' I say to Karin. 'I'm going to walk with you.' She tries to lift me up, but it is an absolute disaster. I am crippled and can't stand at all. Then I say, 'Okay, I'm going to crawl behind you,' but I can't even crawl one step. Finally admitting defeat, I say to her, 'I'm afraid you are on your own. It's getting late now. Go for the camp.'

Karin sets off at about 5:30 p.m. for the camp, to try to get help for the rest of us.

As I lie in the dark next to the crashed helicopter, Rob, who is still trapped in the cockpit, is in serious difficulty. I can see him through the shattered Perspex windscreen. 'I can't breathe, I can't breathe,' he repeats over and over. At one point he is in so much pain that he begs me to end his life with a shot from the revolver I am carrying.

'Just hang in there, Rob, we'll get out of this,' I try to reassure him, although in truth I am not convinced that we will ever get out of this mess.

Elmon and Willie are still lying on the ground, moaning. I have no idea how badly they are injured. I try to speak to them but they don't reply.

Rob, Elmon and Willie are in survival mode, but my mind is sharp and focused. A million ideas are spinning around in my head of how we are going to get out of this predicament; I am in overdrive. There is just one problem – I can't move.

'Can you feel your toes, Rob?' I ask.

'No, nothing!' he replies weakly. My heart sinks. If his spinal cord is severed, he will never walk again. I ask Elmon and Willie the same question. All they can manage is a groan. We are all in serious physical trouble. All our hopes are pinned on Karin.

At about 7:30 p.m. I hear the first shot. My spirits lift immediately. This means that Karin has reached the camp and alerted the game scouts. She will have told the world that we're in trouble, and we will be rescued.

Throughout my career as a cameraman I have carried a .44 Smith & Wesson revolver strapped to my waist. A rifle is too big and cumbersome when I'm trying to carry cameras and make movies. Now I am grateful that I have the revolver. I fire back to help the scouts pinpoint our position. After several shots are exchanged, the four scouts eventually manage to find us. They have Trish Parsons, Rob's wife, with them.

Zambian game scouts are some of the nicest guys I've ever met in my life, but many of them are not very well trained. None of the scouts that have come to rescue us have any knowledge of first aid at all. Their initial instinct is to pull Rob out of the cockpit, but I know that this could be very dangerous for him.

I call the scouts to my side and, by the light of a torch, with my gun in my hand, I have the following conversation with them:

JV: 'You see my gun?'

Scouts: 'We see your gun, JV.'

JV: 'You know it works, don't you?'

Scouts: 'We know it works, JV; you've just fired it.'

JV: 'Now, if anyone pulls Rob out of the cockpit roughly, I will shoot them. Understood?'

Scouts: 'Understood!'

I then give them detailed instructions on how to link arms to lift Rob up and out of the cockpit and lay him gently on the ground.

With the light of a torch on my face and a gun in my hand, I must look pretty fearsome, even though I am lying helpless on the ground. The scouts' faces are grey and their brows are beaded with sweat as they listen attentively to every word I say.

* * *

There were many heroes involved in that horrendous helicopter crash, but none more so than Lloyd Gumede, one of my film assistants from Londolozi.

When Karin arrived at camp after her epic seven-kilometre walk, she asked Lloyd to go and fetch the doctor from Mfuwe, which was a three-hour drive from our camp. To fetch the doctor Lloyd needed to wade across the Luangwa River in the dark, an exceedingly dangerous manoeuvre in a river that boasts over a dozen crocs per mile, and when crocs are particularly active at night … especially for a short guy like Lloyd!

Lloyd made the crossing safely and took the jeep that was parked on the other side to Mfuwe. I had taught Lloyd to drive only about three weeks before this, so he was by no means an experienced driver, and his coordination is not great. He fetched the one and only doctor in Mfuwe, a Swiss mission doctor, who insisted on following in his own car. Lloyd also fetched John Knowles, one of my film assistants.

When Lloyd, John and the doctor reached the Luangwa River some time after midnight, the doctor took one look at the dark, foreboding river that was about three-quarters full and some 200 metres wide, and announced, 'Not for me, boys. I am out of here!'

John asked him if he could provide some painkillers for us, but the doctor just said, 'You have wasted my time. Nobody can cross that river!' And he took off, without so much as leaving an aspirin for us!

Lloyd and John, who is even shorter than Lloyd, then waded back through the crocodile-infested water and arrived at the crash site at 2:30 in the morning.

'Where's the doctor?' I asked John.

'Gone,' he answered.

'Gone where?' I demanded desperately.

'Home,' said John.

'Do you have any painkillers?'

'None.'

Rob, who was in a very bad way by this stage, then asked, 'Do you have whisky?'

'No,' John replied.

Nothing else was said; nothing could be said. It was freezing cold by now, and the pain – everyone's pain now that the adrenalin had worn off – was really bad. Silence reigned over the crash site.

In retrospect, I think both John Knowles and especially Lloyd Gumede should have received bravery awards for their selfless actions that night. To cross the Luangwa River in the daytime is an achievement; to wade across at night, when visibility is poor and the crocodiles are bolder, is sheer madness.

At camp, after sending Lloyd to fetch John and the doctor, Karin had radioed Yusuf Patel, our Zambian partner, who is very well connected politically. She told him that I had gone down in a serious helicopter crash, giving him the coordinates she'd written down. And then the radio's battery died.

Yusuf was another hero that night. After he received Karin's radio message, he leapt into action. First he contacted General Christian Tembo, the Zambian Minister of Tourism, who is a friend of mine. General Tembo in turn organised with the Minister of Defence to fly Zambian air-force helicopters to the crash site.

Through ingenuity and persistence, Yusuf also managed to track down my brother, Dave. Yusuf got hold of a telephone operator in Cape Town – in those days, you had to place international calls through an operator – and asked her where he could find Dave Varty. Incredibly, the operator knew that Dave Varty owned Londolozi Game Reserve. So she got through to the telephone exchange at Skukuza in the Kruger National Park, and they phoned Londolozi. The person who answered the phone at Londolozi said that Dave wasn't there; he was conducting a motivational workshop with staff at a lodge in the Drakensberg mountains.

The operator connected Yusuf to this lodge, and a waiter went over to Dave, who was in the middle of a meal. 'Telephone for you,' he said. 'It's urgent.'

Yusuf told Dave that I had been involved in a helicopter crash and that he didn't know if there were any survivors. Yusuf gave him the coordinates of the crash. Dave never went back to finish his meal. Instead, he sprang into action, phoning Medical Rescue International (MRI) and saying, 'I want you to send two jets, with doctors and all the medical equipment.' They told him that, before they would do anything, he had to deposit R50 000 into their bank account. So in the middle of the night, in the days before internet banking, Dave tried desperately to arrange for the transfer. At first light, the money was transferred, and the two jets took off from Lanseria Airport to fly to Mfuwe.

* * *

We lay at the crash site for eighteen hours. The temperature went from freezing at night to baking hot at midday. Finally I heard the sound of the first helicopter coming from North Luangwa National Park. It was Mark Owens, a friend of mine (and co-author of *Cry of the Kalahari*) who had been contacted by General Tembo. Later, the Zambian air force arrived with paramedics to airlift us to Mfuwe.

One of the paramedics had a camera with him, and as he got out of the chopper he was snapping away. The pictures were later splashed all over the first issue of the *Sunday Independent*, which had just launched.

Although Rob was the worst hurt of all of us, he insisted that the paramedics sort the rest of us out first. When we were all safely strapped in, with neck braces, the air-force choppers took us to Mfuwe, where the MRI jets were waiting to pick us up.

So impressive is modern technology, and such was the efficiency of the rescue, that Rob and I were in intensive care at Milpark Hospital in Johannesburg that same night. Elmon and Willie, who had suffered compressed vertebrae, and Karin, who had injuries to her upper spine, were all admitted to high care at the same hospital.

That night President Nelson Mandela happened to be visiting

a patient in the bed next to mine in the intensive care unit. I had got to know Nelson Mandela quite well when he had visited Londolozi after his release from prison.

Ever perceptive, Madiba saw my name above the bed and immediately went to the doctor to ask about the severity of my injuries. Although I was heavily drugged, I do remember Nelson Mandela's voice saying softly, 'John, I have spoken to the doctor. You will recover, but you must be patient. You will be in hospital for eight to ten weeks. Be strong, my brother.'

The next morning the nurses showed me a snapshot of the great man bending over me, talking into my ear.

I had injuries to my lower spine, and it was indeed eight weeks that I lay on my bed in hospital. Gill and our little daughter, Savannah, visited me every day. I had many hours to contemplate my life and the direction I was going. I came to the conclusion that life is very fragile. I had used at least two of my nine lives in Luangwa – the first was when the five lionesses attacked Shingalana and me, and the second was in the helicopter crash. My decision then was to live faster and more fully, as though every day was my last.

But first I had to learn to walk again. After lying in bed for six weeks, my legs had atrophied. Every day Gill and the nurses helped me onto my feet and I would take a few steps.

No fewer than three orthopaedic surgeons examined me. Two said I should have a back operation and one said I should do nothing – let nature heal your wounds, he advised. Needless to say, I took the advice of the third surgeon. However, he warned that I would be able to film for only ten more years and then my film career would be over. The crash occurred in 1995. At the time of writing, it is fifteen years later and I still film every day of my life. The flexibility of my spine is gone, I have arthritis creeping into the compressed vertebrae, and at the end of a hard day's filming I have pain in my lower back, but I am alive, healthy and living life to the full.

One day, while I was still in hospital, Rob Parsons was wheeled into my ward. It was the first time we'd had a chance to speak to each other since the crash. We discussed what had gone wrong with the helicopter to cause it to crash. We discovered that mechanical failure, not poachers, had been the root cause of the accident.

There is no doubt that Rob's brilliant flying saved all our lives. He had crashed upright, he had prevented a fire and, ironically, he was the worst hurt in the accident (I looked at an X-ray of his back and could clearly see that his spinal cord had nearly been severed). During the rescue he had shown great bravery and self-lessness.

Rob stayed in hospital for eight weeks. He had one back operation, then a second and, finally, a year later, when he was still in excruciating pain, a third. During the third operation complications set in and Rob never recovered consciousness.

A better, braver pilot and friend one could never hope to find. The Eagle in the Sky was gone.

I later wrote a song that I dedicated to Rob Parsons.

> My mind is numb in the darkness
> Pain is my brother tonight
> I give thanks for the skill
> of Rob Parsons, for Elmon, for Karin, for life.
>
> – from 'Eagle in the Sky'

10

Living Dangerously

In 1983, Londolozi was hit by a severe drought that dragged on for many months. Buffalo were one of the worst-hit species and the herds started to fracture – herds normally numbering several hundred were reduced to ten- or fifteen-strong. The animals' pelvic bones were sticking through their skin, and they were lethargic as they battled to find grass to eat.

On the advice of scientists at the Kruger National Park, the decision was reached to cull the starving buffalo. Sabi Sand – which incorporates Londolozi, Mala Mala and the other privately owned farms of the area – is run by an executive committee that asked me to do the culling.

In the Kruger National Park, culling is normally done from a helicopter. Since we didn't have one, we had to do it from the ground. We'd get close to the targeted herd – they were so weak that we could get quite close up – and I would fire a dart filled with scoline, a drug that causes respiratory failure, into the first buffalo's rump. Elmon would pass me the second dart gun and load the third while I fired the second. Within a few minutes of being shot, the buffalo were dead.

We would dart five buffalo at a time and distribute the meat to the surrounding communities – we couldn't cope with more meat than that. The Kruger National Park, by contrast, has an abattoir and is able to process far larger quantities of meat.

After we'd been culling for a few weeks, the state veterinarian, Roy Bengis, who is a friend of mine, said he'd like to come out to see how it was going. He watched us going through our paces, darting the five buffalo, and he seemed quite impressed with the process.

The next day, Elmon and I and four other Shangaan guys went out to cull buffalo. As I removed my darts, I was vaguely aware that Roy had put my darts away in a different way from the method I usually used. Then, as I pulled the plastic cover off one dart, the needle jerked back into my hand. I was instantly terrified: had some of the concentrated scoline, which kills an enormous buffalo within minutes, got into my blood stream? Just a tiny drop would be enough to finish me off. Is this the way my life is going to end, I wondered.

'You know how lethal this drug is?' I said to Elmon. 'You've been culling with me for weeks now.'

'I know, JV. Isn't there an antidote?'

I don't know of any antidote to scoline and, even if there is one, we didn't have it. The guys were all standing around me in a circle, their eyes wide, waiting for me to collapse. Elmon was desperately trying to think of what to do.

A minute passed, and another minute, and I was still feeling fine. To my great relief, I realised that I had struck it lucky – the drug had somehow failed to get into my system.

Then my sense of drama kicked in and I started staggering

around. I fell on the ground and writhed about, as if in agony. I was having a great time, acting for my audience, who were convinced that they were witnessing the death of JV. I looked up and saw their worried faces, and I couldn't control myself; I started to laugh. When they realised that it had all been a joke, they were not amused – my joke had gone down like a lead balloon. I thought that when they saw I was all right they would laugh and join in the joke, but it seriously backfired on me.

The guys all went into a huddle. After a while, Elmon came back and told me solemnly that they didn't want to work any more that day: they took what had happened as a sign that an accident was going to take place. When we got back to camp, the group flatly refused to carry on working and Elmon said that they recommended I go to a witch doctor: 'Because, for sure, if you go out and do another culling, you will be killed, either by a buffalo or by some other accident.'

I never did see the witch doctor. A few days later the rains came, and I abandoned the culling. Luckily, we have never had to cull again since then, or I might have had to pay a visit to the witch doctor first.

* * *

Buffalo featured prominently in another dangerous episode of mine, when Elmon and I were hunting in the Masai Mara with a Masai hunter by the name of Karino Sukuli.

Karino was carrying only a bow and poisoned arrows, and Elmon and I had nothing but our cameras. After a short walk, we found a buffalo bull feeding in a dry river bed. To my surprise, Karino began to stalk towards a medium-sized tree rather than in the direction of the buffalo.

Suddenly the buffalo spun around and charged us. In a flash, Karino was up the tree, and Elmon quickly followed. I was left on the ground to face the music. The buffalo targeted Elmon, who was hanging from a low branch just above horn height. The charging bull repeatedly tried to hook him out of the tree: each time the horns struck the canvas camera bag that Elmon was carrying on his back.

I watched as Elmon's arms began to tire; I wondered how long he could hang on.

The buffalo bull suddenly decided to abandon his attack on Elmon, turning his attention on me. The only thing separating the buffalo from me was the trunk of the tree. The buffalo went left as I went right, in a game of Ring-a-Ring o' Roses. I was intent on making sure that the trunk of the tree stayed between us. In a callous moment, I half-wished Elmon would fall out of the tree so that the buffalo would get him and not me.

Then the bull stopped circling and fixed his gaze on me. I immediately understood exactly what the expression 'a buffalo looks at you as though you owe him money' means. In my case, it seemed to be a very large sum of money – the buffalo's eyes had a particularly evil glint.

Suddenly, the buffalo charged, and as he did so his left horn caught the tree trunk. For a split second, he stumbled. This was the break I needed: I dropped the camera and ran down a narrow path lined with acacia whistling thorn. Close behind me the buffalo was making a blowing sound as it tried to close the gap between us. As the path approached the dry river bed, it split into two. I pretended to move left and then ran along the right-hand path. The buffalo fell for my trick and thundered down the left path. I had narrowly escaped being gored – perhaps even killed – by a raging buffalo bull.

When Karino descended from the tree (Elmon had fallen down by this point), he started to laugh. For a full ten minutes he laughed; the tears rolled down his cheeks. Elmon and I didn't find the incident quite as hilarious as Karino did.

Karino then gave us a lecture on how to sham dead when a buffalo attacks you. Apparently one of his hunting friends had tried to wrestle a buffalo and the buffalo had flicked its horn through him, killing him instantly.

'And where were you when this happened?' I asked Karino.

'I was in a tree,' he replied proudly.

Another hunting friend of Karino's had lain on the ground for thirty minutes pretending to be dead. The buffalo had trampled him, breaking some ribs, but he had not been able to get a horn into him. Finally, believing the man to be dead, the buffalo had ambled off. Karino's friend had got away, and had gone on to make a complete recovery.

'You never shoot a buffalo from the ground,' said Karino. 'It's too dangerous. You only shoot it from a tree.'

For the first time I understood why Karino had stalked towards the tree and not towards the buffalo.

'Next time choose a bigger tree so I can climb in as well,' I said to him.

* * *

In 1990 I went with Elmon and Lynne Richardson, one of my film assistants, to the Peruvian Amazon. We were in search of the jaguar, to make the film *Swift and Silent*, in which we compare the jaguar, the cheetah and the leopard. I funded this movie with my American Express credit card, flying around South America and raising $1000 at a time from different American Express offices – they didn't have computers then so had no record of my withdrawals.

At the end of six fascinating weeks in Peru's Manu National Park, I had organised for a light aircraft to pick us up and take us to the other great jaguar area, the Pantanal in Brazil. On the day we were due to be picked up, we found the pilot, to whose charter company I had already paid $5000, waiting next to his plane at the jungle airstrip. With a big grin on his face, he informed me that the bandits had held him up the day before and taken all his fuel. He looked very relaxed for a man who had just been attacked by bandits, and I was convinced that it was a scam. I tried all my persuasive powers, but it was hopeless – this pilot was not going to fly us to the Pantanal and he had no intention of refunding my money.

The pilot informed me that if I went to a town called Puerto Maldonado I could catch a scheduled flight to Lima. The problem with this plan was that Puerto Maldonado was a three-day boat trip away, and there was only one flight a week out of the town.

We climbed into our boat and began the three-day journey down the river to Puerto Maldonado. Miraculously, as we set off, fuel appeared from nowhere and the pilot got back in his plane and roared off. I believe that nature deals in strange ways with the devious, however. On the way home to Cuzco, flying in bad weather, the pilot hit the mountain and that was the end of both him and his plane.

Unaware of the plane crash and the fate we had survived, we

reached Puerto Maldonado by boat and were informed that the weekly flight would depart the following Wednesday.

We booked our tickets for the flight and arrived at the airport on the designated day to catch our plane. We checked our cameras and six weeks of unique footage, including a rare jaguar sequence, into the cargo hold.

When the doors of the aeroplane opened, I noticed people running across the tarmac to the plane. Some had chickens on their heads, while others had bags of potatoes. This will be an interesting flight, I thought. We strolled across the tarmac to the plane, but, as we reached the top of the stairs of the gangway, the door of the aeroplane was slammed shut in our faces and the aircraft taxied away with our cameras and film footage in its hold. It became obvious that we had been tricked. Our tickets had been resold to the locals, who were now on their way to Lima – in our seats. I was gutted. Frantically I asked if there were any other planes scheduled to take off for our destination. 'Not for a week!' was the reply.

Standing on the runway was a two-seater Cessna light plane. 'Whose plane is that?' I enquired.

'The postal service's,' was the response.

'Where's the pilot?' I asked.

'He's over at the hangar,' I was told. I knocked on the pilot's door and asked if he would fly me to Lima. I flashed $1 000 in front of him with the promise of another $1 000 when he got me there. This was a huge amount of Peruvian pesos.

In broken English he explained that he didn't fly to Lima and neither did the plane – it was too small. In desperation, I produced another $1 000. This changed his mind immediately. 'Actually, my friend can fly you to Lima. Wait here!' he commanded.

The pilot returned with the most dubious-looking character I have ever seen – he looked like a cross between Che Guevara and Frankenstein's monster.

'Can you fly this plane?' I asked him anxiously.

'Yes,' he replied.

Not convinced, I asked, 'Do you have a licence?'

'Only ask him if he can fly,' responded the pilot. 'Don't ask him if he has a licence.'

The next morning a scary-looking unlicensed Peruvian pilot and I took off in a small plane, in an attempt to fly over the Andes to Lima. Elmon and Lynne stayed another week in Puerto Maldonado before catching the next scheduled flight out to join me. The first thing I noticed when we were airborne was that the plane's fuel gauges were not working. This has to be one of the dumbest things I have ever done in my life, I thought to myself.

An hour into the flight it became turbulent, whereupon the pilot informed me he wasn't feeling well and that I should steer the aircraft. What kept crossing my mind was the story of the football team that had crashed in the Andes. To survive, some of the passengers had eaten the flesh of those who had died in the crash. Looking at Frankenstein's monster puking into his packet, I decided that I would rather starve to death than eat him.

How we reached Lima in one piece, God only knows, but we did.

With the Peruvian pilot translating, I asked where my cameras and film might be. I fully expected that I would have to pay a hefty bribe to get my equipment back, but an airport official calmly unlocked an office and there stood my cameras and film, intact and unharmed!

After I'd paid the pilot his $3 000, he quietly told me that he had done the flight many times before when he regularly flew marijuana and other drugs from the jungle to Lima.

* * *

In the mid-nineties I was making the film *River Dinosaur – A Crocodile Safari in Africa* in the South Luangwa National Park. One day I was travelling down the Luangwa River in a long, thin wooden 'banana boat' when I came upon a sub-adult elephant bull that had drowned in the water. I decided to tow it back to my camp so that I could film the crocodiles feeding on it. It took most of the day to get it back to camp, where I tied it to a tree with a thick rope.

That night a huge crocodile arrived and began ripping at the carcass, and others swiftly followed. I filmed a sequence of crocs feeding on land. In the morning, I found that the rope had broken and that the elephant carcass had drifted down the Luangwa River to a point some 300 metres away from the camp.

Determined to get my carcass back, I went down the river in my boat and stopped next to it. Presuming that the crocs had left, I stepped out of the boat and onto the back of the dead elephant to tie a rope to it. To my horror, the carcass began to move further out into the river. The large crocodile from the night before, an elephant leg in his mouth, was still there: he was not going to give up his carcass easily and was swimming strongly towards the river's middle.

Perched precariously on the back of a greasy, bloody and very slippery dead elephant, I found myself being towed by a huge crocodile out into the middle of the Luangwa River, which is about 300 metres wide in full flood.

Panic set in. I screamed for help. Elmon, who was back at camp, and Richard Jones, another cameraman, heard my calls. They immediately ran for the inflatable boat, which took a while to start. All the while, I continued my hazardous journey on the back of the dead elephant.

Eventually Elmon and Richard managed to steer the rubber duck alongside the moving elephant and I was able to step into the boat to safety. The crocodile got its prize and I was thankful to get away with my life. I'd used up another of my precious nine lives.

* * *

An old bull hippo in the Luangwa River caused us many problems while we were filming in the area. We had to move through his territory to get to our camp, and this old bull had got into the habit of charging the banana boat as we crossed the river.

One day I was alone in the boat when the bull charged from the water. I stood up at the back of the vessel, planning to bang the oars on the sides of the boat to frighten the hippo. As I stood up, my revolver caught the throttle of the 50-horsepower Mariner engine, opening the engine to full revs. The boat reared up, and both the engine and I fell off the back into the river.

The engine quickly sank to the bottom of the river, but the rubber fuel line stretched without breaking, anchoring the boat in the middle of the Luangwa River.

There was no way I could swim for land through that density of crocodiles, so I decided to climb back into the boat to empty the fuel tank, leaving it as a buoy above the sunken engine. Being a good conservationist, I didn't want to pollute the Luangwa River with the fuel, so I emptied it into the bottom of the boat and left the empty fuel tank marking the spot where the engine had sunk.

Somehow, as I drifted down the river, I managed to get some fuel on my private parts. In agony, I jumped back out of the boat and hung onto the side, hoping that the water would ease the pain and that I wouldn't be eaten by crocs. The banana boat drifted silently with the current and, after three kilometres, it hit a sandbank. Several hours later, John Knowles and some scouts arrived to rescue me.

As we stood on the river bank planning how to get our engine back, Robert Banda, one of the scouts, simply waded into the river, reached down into the water, pulled the engine out and loaded it into the boat. Whether it was bravado because he had a number of scouts looking on or whether it was complete foolhardiness, I will never know. One thing I do know though is that you have to be incredibly brave to wade into shoulder-deep water in the middle of the crocodile-infested Luangwa River, let alone pick up a sixty-kilogram engine from the depths of the river bed.

It is a testimony to Mariner engines that after we put the rescued engine on the bank, drained the oil and left it in the sun for an hour, it started first time.

A second hippo played a part in a drama in which I think I used up another of my lives. While we were driving down a remote part of the Luangwa River, I noticed a dead hippo lying on a sandbank in the middle of the river. I had filmed an outstanding sequence of crocodiles hunting and killing seventeen gazelles out of a herd of twenty-two in the Mara River the year before, and I wanted a frenzy of crocodiles feeding off a hippo for my crocodile film. The problem was that the hippo was too far away for my filming lights to reach it, and I knew the crocodiles would congregate after dark.

I decided to use the cable from my winch, attach it to a rope and use the jeep to pull the hippo closer to the bank, where I could film with lights in the dark. Leaving my revolver with the scouts, I waded out to attach the rope to the dead hippo.

The Luangwa River is deceptive: what looks like shallow water can suddenly become deep as hidden channels criss-cross the river bed. I started wading out, ankle, knee, waist and then neck deep, until finally I was swimming. This is madness, I told myself – but at that stage I was closer to the hippo than I was to the mainland, so I pushed on. When I reached the dead hippo, I began the tricky job of roping the smelly three-ton carcass, which took me longer than anticipated.

Now, if I could wade back with the rope that was attached to the dead hippo, I could pull the hippo close to the bank and my film lights would be able to capture the frenzy of feeding that was a vital sequence in my documentary on crocodiles.

The best-laid plans can and do go wrong, however. As I began my journey back to land and the jeep, I noticed that a large crocodile had positioned itself between me and the jeep: the crocodile had cut me off from the mainland. As the sun began to set across the Luangwa River, I sat unarmed next to a smelly dead hippo. Never did a sunset look so ugly.

I shouted to the scouts to shoot the crocodile, which they were not allowed to do as we were in a national park, where all animals are protected. They fired shots at the big croc but it dropped under the water, only to emerge later even closer to where I was positioned with the dead hippo. As darkness approached, I found myself surrounded by a dozen hungry crocodiles, all becoming bolder by the minute. The situation was dire, and panic began to set in.

Then, just as things were looking hopeless, I saw a small light on an approaching boat. It was a fisherman coming down the river with a paraffin lantern in his boat. I called to him and he responded. He was very agitated, telling me that just an hour before, as he had been pulling in his fishing nets, a large crocodile had hit the fish in the nets, nearly overturning him into the water. I pointed out my predicament but he insisted that there was no way his small fishing boat could get the two of us off that island. I weigh about seventy kilograms and he must have weighed roughly the same, and our combined weight would be likely to sink the boat.

I was desperate ... I have never negotiated so hard in my life. I bought his boat. I bought the nets, which he agreed to leave on the island. I bought all the fish he had caught. I offered him around US$700 in kwacha, which for a fisherman then was a fortune. It was the best deal I have ever made in my entire life.

As I climbed into the tiny fishing boat, I thought to myself: Is this the end of the road for JV? Is this where, on a remote part of the Luangwa River, JV and a brave unknown fisherman meet their end?

I started planning my epitaph: 'He was too bold, too reckless. He understood big cats but not crocodiles. RIP.'

Finally, while I lay across the fisherman's boat, delicately balanced like a sack of corn, my head in the water on one side and my feet dangling over the other, the fisherman manoeuvred the boat ever so slowly between the waiting crocs. From my position

I was eyeball to eyeball with the crocs, and I didn't like what I saw. Primitive, patient, the crocs waited for one false move. Neither of us said a word; all that could be heard was the swishing of the oar. Although the distance we covered was only 200 metres, it took us a good fifteen minutes to get to the mainland, certainly the longest fifteen minutes of my life. Instinctively, the fisherman knew that he had both his own life and my life in his hands, and he responded magnificently, inching us across the dark water with great skill.

In retrospect, his actions were some of the bravest I have ever encountered. The water was millimetres from the top of the boat. Most of the fishermen in the park cannot swim, so had one of the crocs had a go at my trailing head or feet, it would have been disaster for the fisherman and me.

It was dark when we landed on the mainland, yet even in the dark I could see the sombre, grey faces of the scouts. They knew they had almost witnessed a tragedy.

As I turned the lights of the jeep onto the dead hippo, I could already see twenty hungry crocs ripping at the carcass. I had missed a great shot, but I had survived, and that's all that mattered.

Later, when I paid the fisherman his money, he told me that he had never been in that part of the river before and he would never go back there. It is a dangerous place, he said, and the crocs are very aggressive. I agreed with him wholeheartedly. I estimated that my chances of someone coming along that day had been less than one in a thousand. Once again, Mother Nature had smiled upon me.

* * *

One night I was hunting with the tigers Ron and Julie, whom I'd acquired in 2000 (see Chapter 15). In order to get the tigers back-lit, I had a second lighting vehicle, which had a generator in the back, to power the filming lights.

Sitting in the front of the vehicle were my two film assistants, Andries, who was driving, and Johannes. In the back of the truck next to the generator was a guy called Sammy. It was Sammy's first time out – he had never seen a tiger before and knew nothing about film making. Unaware of the danger from the fumes, he had started the generator and closed all the windows. After a short while, I had a puncture in the jeep I was driving, so I called on the radio for Andries to bring the lighting vehicle to help me.

When they arrived, there was no sign of Sammy. I asked Andries where he was, and he replied that Sammy was scared of the tigers so he was lying flat. This seemed a bit strange, so I opened the back of the truck and there lay Sammy, unconscious: the fumes of the generator had knocked him out. I instructed Andries and Johannes to help me pull him out of the truck. Sammy is tall – easily six feet – but weighs no more than sixty kilograms. As we pulled him out, he fell with a thud onto the ground.

The tigers were hunting a good 500 metres away, but they heard the sound and associated it with food. Suddenly, in the light of the spotlight, two sets of tigers' eyes could be seen moving quickly towards us. Andries and Johannes immediately abandoned me and leapt back into the front of the truck. I was left with an uncon-scious Sammy on the ground and two rapidly approaching tigers. Adrenalin is an amazing thing because, single-handedly, somehow I was able to pull Sammy back into the vehicle to safety.

We left the tigers at high speed and pulled up near a dam

several kilometres away. Here I administered mouth-to-mouth resuscitation for fifteen minutes. It seemed to have no effect. I could feel no pulse at all. Andries informed me solemnly that Sammy was dead.

In desperation, I ordered Andries to throw water over Sammy. Eventually I saw the tiniest flicker of an eyelid. I gave Sammy more mouth-to-mouth and more water. We put him next to the window of the truck and drove at high speed to get the wind into his face. Gradually he began to breathe. Later an ambulance took him to hospital, where he made a full recovery.

* * *

On a Friday evening in April 2003 I was flying to Johannesburg, where I had to prepare for a nasty arbitration concerning my tiger project.

On the aeroplane I started talking to some avid wildlife photographers. They invited me to join them – they were heading for a place called Teazers, which they assured me was a lot of fun.

I thoroughly enjoyed the evening, with loads of beautiful women dancing on the tables, although I was informed by a large bouncer that the beautiful women were for viewing only.

After my friends departed, I was heading for my car when out of a dark alley stepped a gorgeous Indian woman. The lady was extremely engaging and asked if I was from out of town. She offered to show me the town, an invitation I found hard to refuse. As I was discussing the possible activities for the night, three police officers stepped out of the dark and arrested me for loitering. There was no doubt in my mind that I had been caught in a sting. As the policemen drove me to the police station, I couldn't help remembering my dad once saying to me, 'Son, sometimes the most beautiful flowers are the most poisonous!'

At the police station I was told that I would be charged, and that I would spend the weekend in jail and appear in the magistrates' court on the following Monday morning. I could just imagine the news headlines as I began the tiger-project arbitration: 'Conservationist arrested for picking up hooker'.

The police officers, who had been drinking, were extremely aggressive and demanded that I sign an admission-of-guilt form. I refused to do it, and tried speaking Shangaan to them, but the most senior of the cops said contemptuously that he hated the language, and that my Shangaan was lousy anyway! In desperation, I pulled out a newspaper cutting, which showed me with a tiger. The cop studied the article intently. The piece made reference to the arbitration. The cop's face lit up, and he banged on the table and announced to the other police officers, 'We have caught a famous thief!'

It was obvious to me that this was all leading to a point where I would pay a substantial bribe in return for walking free. The drunken police officers were somewhat confused, however. I was dressed, as I usually am, in torn, ragged fatigues, and didn't look remotely like a man of means. The police officer asked me if I had any money, and I replied 'No'. He asked where I was staying that night, to which I replied, 'I don't know. I am a stranger to Joburg.'

Just then two more police officers arrived with another man who had been caught in the same sting. All attention shifted to the new guy, who was dripping with gold chains and watches. Now here was some real money, a good chance of getting a fat bribe. After uttering a racial obscenity, the rich guy was marched down to the cells below. They seemed to have completely forgotten about me.

At this point the beautiful Indian woman entered the room. I realised that she was a policewoman and part of the sting operation. She smiled at me and asked if I could take her home. I duly obliged, although I was nervous that this was just another trap. On the way to her house, which was in the south of Johannesburg, she asked me how much I had paid in bribes. I told her that I had not paid anything. She declared that she was going to report the police officers for corruption.

During the trip to her house, I turned on my CD player and Bob Dylan's 'Blowin' in the Wind' came on. I started singing along.

She must have been impressed with my voice, because she asked me if I was a singer. I told her that I was.

'How many records have you made?' she asked.

'Two,' I replied (I didn't tell her that I had actually sold only two records, one to my mother and one to Spike Milligan). She told me about a late-night place that played live music that I would enjoy. Still wary that this might be another sting, I agreed to go along.

We arrived at a barn somewhere in the south of Johannesburg. It looked to me like a shebeen, with bales of hay and sawdust on the floor and some very dodgy-looking people hanging out. The air was thick with marijuana smoke, and from a wooden stage a one-man band entertained the crowd, which seemed to be in a permanent state of euphoria and elevation.

When we entered, the singer immediately put down his guitar

and came over. The policewoman introduced me as a singer, to which the one-man band said, 'Someone is moving in on my chick. Will you take over the singing?'

At 2 a.m., somewhere in the south of Joburg, in a dope-smoked tavern, I played my conservation songs to an audience that probably didn't know the difference between a tortoise and an elephant.

At one point some dope head threw two R5 coins onto the stage in appreciation of my music. I finally knew that, if all else failed in my life, people would pay good money to hear me sing!

The policewoman and I finally left the tavern as the mulberry dawn was appearing over the Joburg skyline. The marijuana smoke had made me light-headed and I felt like I was walking on air. The sunrise looked purple and the police lady particularly beautiful. I understood for the first time what junkies must feel like when they go on a trip.

An hour later I was in an arbitration meeting with three steely-eyed lawyers who were cross-questioning me. Strangely, my memory seemed to have completely deserted me!

There is a poetic twist in this story. Several months later, the TV show *Special Assignment* trapped the police officers I'd encountered that Friday night using hidden cameras. The officers were dismissed from the police force for corruption and taking bribes.

If the policewoman I met that night ever reads this book, would she please make contact with me through my website, www.jvbigcats.co.za? I would dearly love to know if she was the one who blew the whistle on the corrupt cops, and I could also sing her one more song.

11

The Mother Leopard

I am fourteen years old and I am hunting on our family's game farm, Sparta, with Two Tone Sithole, a well-known poacher and superb tracker. We are in an area called Princess Alice's Bush. Two Tone is about 1.6 metres in height, short and stocky with a huge beard like Blackbeard the pirate. Suddenly he stops to listen.

From a distance of half a kilometre away, we hear the distress call of a duiker. In an instant, Two Tone is up and running towards the sound. Carrying a 30-06 Springfield rifle, I am battling to keep up with the swiftly moving tracker.

Suddenly, in a small clearing in the bush, we come across the bleating grey duiker. It is being held by its back leg in the jaws of a black-backed jackal.

We are not the only ones to have heard the duiker's distress call. In anticipation of an easy meal, a large male leopard is racing to the scene. As the leopard arrives, the jackal releases the duiker. Jackal and duiker flee in opposite directions, and the leopard comes to a halt in a cloud of dust.

A shot through the heart from my 30-06 ends the leopard's life. The encounter has been brief, and fatal for the leopard.

Fifteen years later, in 1979, close to where I shot the male leopard, I caught a glimpse of a female leopard. Unlike other leopards, she didn't immediately run but stayed for five or six minutes. I was transfixed by her beauty, her grace, the suppleness of her body and her haunting eyes. For me it was a defining moment, a life-changing event.

I had just acquired a movie camera and I told Elmon that I was going to make a film about this leopard, and that he should help me.

Elmon was dubious. 'How are we going to film an animal that we can't find?' he asked.

'You are going to find her, and I am going to film her,' was my response.

I didn't realise it at the time, but I was about to enter one of the most exciting periods of my life. Over time I would be allowed into the secret world of a female leopard that I simply called 'the Mother Leopard'. At the same time, I would be privileged to witness the incredible skill of a master tracker, Elmon Mhlongo, at work. The journey would take fourteen years.

Our routine was pretty much the same every day. Elmon and I would track the Mother Leopard on foot. If we found her, we would go back to our jeep and try to reach her in the vehicle. Often we would park 100 metres away and then gradually creep closer to her until we were within range to film her.

At times we lost her for weeks, and at one point we presumed her dead. Gradually we were able to habituate the Mother Leopard, which means that, although she remained a wild cat and carried on with her normal life – marking territory, mating, raising young and hunting – she allowed us to follow, film and observe her and, in a way, gave us access to her private life. (Habituation is not to be confused with rehabilitation, which is when a cat that has been raised from young by humans is introduced back into its natural environment.)

When we located her, we would radio the rangers doing the game drives and they would bring their guests in to view and photograph the Mother Leopard. Because she allowed people to get relatively close to her – the first leopard to do so – she quickly became a celebrity, and was the most photographed leopard in the world at that time.

I was determined to capture the first mating leopards on film, but the problem was her mate, who was exceedingly shy.

One night Elmon and I parked 200 metres from the mating leopards. We shone a spotlight onto the animals for no more than three seconds at a time, hoping we could get the male used to the light. It was painstaking work, but, finally, at one in the morning, we were in range to roll a shot of the mating leopards. Unfortunately, during the habituation process, we had used up all of our battery power. The filming lights were now too dim and it was impossible to make a shot. We raced back to camp, turned on the generator that powered Londolozi in those days and charged up all the batteries on the quickest possible charge.

When we got back to the leopards, we manoeuvred ourselves into position and waited for them to start mating again (this happens every fifteen to twenty minutes for a period of three days). At the critical moment, just as the male mounted the female, the batteries caught fire – the entire lighting rig went up in smoke, and the male leopard bolted. In our haste to charge the batteries, we had set the charger too high and had cooked them. It was now three in the morning and time was of the essence: we knew that once the sun came up the male leopard would disappear and we would have lost our once-in-a-lifetime shot.

Back at camp, we hastily replaced the burnt batteries with new ones and sped back to the leopards. The male seemed fatigued and was sleeping soundly near the Mother Leopard, who also seemed to have lost interest. Was the mating over, I wondered.

An hour passed and the first signs of sunrise began to appear on the horizon. I was gutted that I had missed a unique sequence due to some bad luck and bad management on our part.

Suddenly the Mother Leopard got up, circled her mate, sat down on his head to wake him up, and circled him again, emitting a strange purring sound. She then presented in front of him. The male was so tired that he ignored the filming lights and mounted the Mother Leopard. Although the camera registered no light, I had an image and rolled the shot of the mating leopards.

Later, I told the film lab to push the shot two stops during processing. The result was a grainy but clear image of mating leopards, the first ever captured on film. Elmon had recorded the sound on a tape recorder. I was elated.

I have filmed many leopards mating since that initial sequence, but that first one is still the most special by far.

By 1982 we were finding the Mother Leopard on a regular basis and she continued to expose many unique and interesting facts about leopard behaviour to us.

The Mother Leopard gave birth to a litter of cubs, one male and one female, in July that year. I called the female 'Sunset Female' because she set up her territory on the periphery of her mother's territory, in an area called Sunset Bend.

At the beginning of 1988, Sunset Female gave birth to one cub. In May of that year, she and the cub contracted the life-threatening sarcoptic mange. Some of the rangers at Londolozi suggested that I tranquillise her and the cub to treat the mange and save their lives.

Heated discussions and arguments followed, but I steadfastly refused to intervene. My argument was that mange was a natural process and therefore should be left to take its natural course. If Sunset Female had been caught in a wire snare or something else man-made, I would certainly have intervened.

In June that year, both Sunset Female and her cub died. Her death had a profound effect on me. Here was a fellow creature born at Londolozi, relaxed and very viewable, teaching us many new facts about leopards. I had let her die when I'd had it in my power to help her.

I began to see the Mother Leopard in a new light. I started viewing her as an ambassador leopard who, through her relaxed temperament, was bridging the gap between humans and leopards.

Could it be that, instinctively, the Mother Leopard knew that her best chance of survival lay in a partnership with human beings?

Years later, when a granddaughter of the Mother Leopard, Manana 3:4, and her two cubs contracted mange, I was very quick to pull out a dart gun and treat her and her cubs, extending Manana 3:4's life by thirteen years.

Today my outlook is very different from what it was then. I now see leopards as individuals with different personalities. Some will always be shy and elusive, while others are prepared to share their lives with us in symbiotic relationships. It is these ambassador leopards that have slowly and surely revealed the secret world of the leopard to us, and the Mother Leopard was the first.

The ambassador leopards have been photographed thousands and thousands of times over, bringing people from all over the world to Africa, to places like Londolozi, to view, photograph and admire the African leopard.

One field of understanding that was opened up to us by the Mother Leopard was that of the inter-predator aggression that exists between the lion, the leopard, the cheetah, the spotted hyena and the wild dog.

In January 1983, the Mother Leopard produced a litter of three cubs. While she was away hunting one day, she left them in a dry river bed. A group of lions came upon the cubs and killed two of them, leaving one. This was the first inkling we had that there was aggression or regulation between these two species of predators.

During a period of grieving, the Mother consumed parts of the dead cubs and hoisted them into trees. Throughout this grieving period she continued to call for her dead cubs.

In December 1988, the Mother would take the burial of a cub one step further. She had a litter of two cubs, and the male was a little too bold. When he was quite big – four months old – he was also killed by lions. The Mother Leopard took his body up into a tree and fed on it for several hours, and then she buried the rest of his body in the sand in the dry river bed. She had removed all trace of the dead cub so that the hyenas couldn't get at him, and she remained in the area, calling for him, for another four days. After that she seemed to have achieved closure.

The Mother Leopard taught me about the range of emotions

that leopards feel. Like us, they experience grief and go through a mourning period after a loss.

More recently at Tiger Canyons I have seen Shadow consume her dead cub and Julie consume parts of the body and then bury the remainder. All the work that I've done with leopards has helped me to understand the behaviour of tigers, as the two species are similar in many ways. Both leopards and tigers undergo a period of grieving, then removal of the body by consumption, and sometimes even burial of the remaining body parts. It is a moving, emotional ceremony, not unlike the funeral of a human being.

As a film maker, I have to remain objective when I'm following a big cat with which I have a relationship. It is my job to record what I'm observing. So I capture it on film, after which I have to interpret it and, finally, I have to communicate it as best I can.

Leopards can live for up to seventeen years in the wilds, but few will attain this age. The fact is that they live violent lives and very often their deaths are violent. By 1990 the Mother Leopard was estimated to be fourteen years old already. She had produced an incredible eighteen cubs that I knew of, and the next one, her nineteenth – a male born in October 1992 – did not disperse from her as male cubs usually do, but stayed with his aged mother.

To ensure a strong gene pool, at the age of between fourteen and twenty months old, a female cub disperses from her mother and forms a territory adjacent to hers. Male cubs typically move further away from their mother to establish their own territories.

Could it be that this male cub and the Mother Leopard knew instinctively that she was becoming more and more vulnerable to attacks from lions and hyenas? If he stayed with his elderly mother for longer, he could catch prey for her and help her hoist food into trees.

By 1993, the Mother Leopard had noticeably slowed and she lacked the agility to jump into trees to escape from attacking lions and hyenas. And so it was that one day I found her badly ripped up by lions.

My first thought was to call for a vet to try to treat her wounds. Then I thought, what help would that be? The wounds were huge and she was sixteen years old. I knew it was the end of the road for the Mother Leopard.

I sat on the ground six metres from her and cried. I had been with her for fourteen years of her life and now our time was ending. Then, as I sat there feeling sorry for myself, it occurred to me that the least I could do was give her some comfort during the last hours of her life.

I went back to camp and fetched some impala meat and water. Returning to the Mother Leopard, I sat down on the ground near her, offering her the meat and the water. I was shocked as she got to her feet and hobbled towards me – her wounds were truly terrible. Then, with dignity and grace, she sat two metres from me and ate the meat and drank the water.

The tears rolled down my cheeks as emotion overwhelmed me. Time stood still at Londolozi.

After she had finished the food and water, the Mother Leopard limped into the shade of a tree a few metres away from me, stretched out and went to sleep. I think she was glad I was there, if for nothing else than the protection I provided. I too dozed off and, when I awoke, she had not moved. I moved across to her, but there was no movement. I presumed she was dead.

Thoughts raced through my head. Should I bury her? Should I leave her for the hyenas? Should I mount her body for posterity? Confusion and sadness clouded my mind. As I stood contemplating what to do, the Mother Leopard lifted her head off the ground: she was still alive, but only just – her breathing was shallow and her eyes sunken. The thought crossed my mind that the kindest thing I could do was to shoot her, but I simply couldn't bring myself to do it.

It was getting late and I decided that I should sleep in my jeep next to her to protect her from prowling hyenas. I went to camp to get my gear for the night and, as I drove back to the Mother Leopard, I got caught in a huge thunderstorm, complete with hail. I returned to camp to wait out the storm. Once the storm had abated I went back, but the Mother Leopard was gone.

Near to where she had lain was a termite mound with several deep burrows. For protection from the storm and hyenas, she had crawled deep into the burrow, and it was there that she had died.

The Mother Leopard taught me many important values that I cherish to this day. She was an excellent mother who defended her cubs courageously and cared for them tenderly. She had strength, speed, beauty and intelligence – all qualities we humans so admire. She spawned an industry of leopards, of which eight generations survive today. She was the first leopard to display trust in human beings, the leopard that opened the secret world of her species to those prepared to wait, listen, watch and learn.

Pictures of the Mother Leopard can be seen all over the world, in many countries and on most continents. Books, poems and songs have been written about her. She is one of the most photographed leopards of all time – I personally shot more than a million feet of film of her and her cubs.

I had not fully realised the impact the Mother Leopard had had on my life, and it took me a long time to recover from her death.

I wrote a song in tribute to her.

> Your eyes are looking through me
> Deep inside my soul
> Your legacy goes on and on
> It never will grow old
>
> A silent bond connects us
> A secret life revealed
> A conscious shift across divide
> A fleeting mystery
> > – from 'You are Beautiful'

She had come into my life in September 1979 and she had taken me on a fascinating journey for the next fourteen years. She had changed the way I thought about leopards and indeed all wild creatures.

She determined the direction that my life would take from that time on: I would live close to big cats – very close!

12

Jamu, the Leopard Orchid

Game scouts patrolling the Luangwa Valley in Zambia one day came across a female leopard that had been caught in a poacher's snare. The leopard had fought against the snare, which had tightened around her neck, throttling her to death.

When the scouts examined the dead leopard's body, they noticed that she was lactating. By following her tracks, they managed to locate a tiny leopard cub hidden in a den. They called her 'Jamu', the name in Nyanja for the beautiful Leopard Orchid flower, which abounds in the Luangwa Valley.

I was at my camp in the Masai Mara in Kenya when the message came from Luangwa that the scouts had rescued the leopard cub. Would I be prepared to reintroduce it into the wilds, I was asked.

It was the rainy season in the Luangwa Valley and the scouts were unreachable by road, so in my banana boat I went down the Luangwa River to Tundwe Camp, where they were keeping the cub.

Jamu was a beautiful female leopard cub, just four weeks old and in perfect condition. She took readily to the bottle of fortified milk and egg yolk I gave her. A leopard mother's milk is very high in fat, so I'd added cream to the solution. Jamu quickly settled down and seemed to accept that her world had changed, and that her future lay in a partnership with human beings, who would be her new family.

Tundwe Camp is a beautiful rustic camp set among magnificent trees on the banks of the Luangwa River. It is owned by a friend of mine, Gulam Patel, a businessman from Lusaka. Gulam had a pet warthog called Ngulia, and she and Jamu soon struck up an unlikely friendship. Watching Ngulia and Jamu play was amusing in itself. Add to the mix my daughter, Savannah, then just three years old, and we had a hilarious comedy of pig, leopard and human being interacting. Set against the stunning backdrop of Tundwe Camp, this was truly a film maker's dream.

As the rainy season drew to a close, we left Ngulia the warthog behind and moved Jamu out to our tented camp on the edge of a beautiful floodplain called Zebra Plain. It was an ideal place to raise a leopard, with open woodlands and dense thickets surrounding the plain. Behind the plain to the south was the great Luangwa River, and in the riverine forest were large herds of impala. Out on the plains were zebra, puku and warthog, all potentially good prey species for leopards.

I selected a film crew to stay with Gill, Savannah and me in the camp at Zebra Plain to record the journey of Jamu being reintroduced into the wilds of the Luangwa Valley. The team consisted of Anton Truesdale, a wildlife film producer, and his wife, Jo, a stills photographer; Richard Jones, a cameraman; and John Knowles, an assistant cameraman. Spending time with these great people in a magnificent place like Luangwa while filming the beautiful Jamu was idyllic. Time meant nothing: days turned to weeks and weeks turned to months as Jamu's fascinating journey unfolded.

You walk a fine line when rehabilitating a leopard in a place like Luangwa. I didn't want to bring up Jamu in a totally protected world. I was anxious to expose her to the dangers of prey animals and rival predators. At the same time, if I allowed her to take too many risks too quickly, she could easily be killed.

Jamu seemed to have no fear. On one occasion, she strode out across the plain towards a herd of zebra. At Londolozi, I had witnessed a zebra chop a young lion with its hooves, breaking the lion's spine. I had been badly bitten by a zebra myself during a capture operation, and I knew them to be formidable opponents – far too dangerous for an inexperienced young leopard.

We watched anxiously as Jamu approached the herd of zebra. The stallion telegraphed his intentions with mock kicks and head tossing. He allowed Jamu to come close and then he charged. Zebras are exceedingly fast – the speed and aggression of the stallion was pitted against the agility of the young leopard. The zebra tried to break Jamu's spine as she ran for the trees, weaving and dodging the flailing hooves. With the zebra intensifying the attack, I ran straight towards it, firing my revolver into the air. My unexpected attack caused the stallion to hesitate momentarily and, in that brief second, Jamu escaped with her life. It had been a close call.

A week later, Jamu again targeted the wrong prey animal. This time it was a territorial male puku. Puku males can weigh up to ninety kilograms and they have sharp horns that could easily spear a young leopard to death. The male puku allowed Jamu to approach before lowering his head and charging her. This time

Jamu didn't run, but decided to dodge the charging puku. Finally, much to our relief, she abandoned the game and retired to the shade of the woodlands.

Richard and Anton had set their Arriflex cameras to 100 frames per second; later, while we were watching the slow-motion pictures, we realised that the puku had come perilously close to stabbing the young leopard several times. Had the puku succeeded in getting a horn in, the result could have been fatal. Once again, Jamu's agility and athleticism had saved her life.

A few weeks after the puku attack, Jamu was spat in the eyes by a Mozambique spitting cobra. I noticed her rubbing her paws over her eyes and we treated her straight away by syringing water and milk into her eyes. She was learning rapidly that fellow creatures could kick, spit, bite and trample her. I too was gaining valuable experience in the dos and don'ts of returning a young leopard to the wilds.

Jamu grew into a beautiful adult leopard, and when she was thirteen months old it was time for her to disperse from the territory around our camp on Zebra Plain. One night a vicious fight broke out a few metres away from Anton and Jo's tent. When Anton went to investigate, he saw a large female leopard disappearing into the bush. Jamu was up an ebony tree, unhurt, but obviously terrified. In the morning, try as we might, we were unable to coax her down – in fact, she remained in the tree for several days.

Gradually Jamu began to disperse from the camp on Zebra Plain and we were all elated that she should be taking this major step to becoming a wild leopard so naturally. To track her movements, we fitted her with a telemetry collar, and for six weeks Jamu moved into a territory adjacent to the camp. This is typically how leopards disperse but, in a normal situation, Jamu would be establishing a territory on the periphery of her mother's territory. Jamu, by contrast, was attempting to establish a territory on the edge of a non-related, aggressive, territorial female leopard.

Luangwa has one of the densest leopard populations in Africa. In retrospect, to expect Jamu to establish a territory in this high density of leopards was too much to ask. What had probably happened was that she had clashed with other territorial female leopards and, lacking the experience or confidence, had returned to her comfort zone near the camp at Zebra Plain. Now she was back in the territory of the large, aggressive female leopard that had attacked her previously.

One night, we heard sounds of a fight from our camp. In the morning, Anton found blood on the grass, a few bones and the chewed remains of Jamu's collar. More than likely the aggressive female had attacked Jamu and injured her. Young and inexperienced, Jamu would have been no match for a big, powerful, territorial leopard. I have come to learn that with both leopards and tigers, the females are more territorial than the males, and will fight viciously for territory.

The fight would have been heard by the opportunistic hyenas and, once they had located the injured Jamu, two or three hyenas would easily have killed her. Unlike a leopard that kills another leopard and leaves its body, hyenas will eat anything, including a dead leopard. All that we ever found of Jamu were those few bones and the chewed-up telemetry collar. It was a sad end to a beautiful leopard who was promising to disperse and become a fully fledged wild leopard.

Looking back, I have no doubt that if we could have raised her in an area with no leopards, or just a few, Jamu would have been successful.

The film *Jamu – The Orphaned Leopard* shows, dramatically, Jamu nearly losing her life to the zebra stallion and almost being speared by the male puku. Her journey to adulthood was both intriguing and exciting, and she inspired all of us with her grace and beauty.

I take solace from the fact that I gave Jamu an extra year of life, for if the scouts had not discovered the orphaned leopard in the den, and if I had not made the journey from the Masai Mara to the Luangwa Valley, Jamu would have starved to death as a tiny four-week-old cub.

Winnis Mathebula, master lion hunter, tracker, storyteller and teacher

Warren Samuels, high-action cameraman, in the Masai Mara

Numbola, personal hunter and tracker of James Stevenson-Hamilton, the first warden of the Kruger National Park, with my brother, Dave

Elmon Mhlongo: tracker, mentor, cameraman and friend

Dr Roy Bengis stitches a lion after removing a wire snare from its neck

Karin Slater, who made the epic walk back to camp to get help after the helicopter crash in Luangwa, Zambia

Lynne Richardson, fellow film maker, with Mozambican refugees in the film *The Crossover*, which explores the Shangaan culture and traditions

Coaching Enoch Mkanzi on how to use an Arriflex movie camera

Minutes after this aerial shot of buffalo was taken, our helicopter
crashed in the South Luangwa National Park

Being evacuated from the helicopter crash site, eighteen hours
after crash-landing in the Zambian bush

Heroic helicopter pilot Rob Parsons and me after eight weeks in hospital following the
helicopter crash. Both of us had to learn to walk again because our legs had atrophied

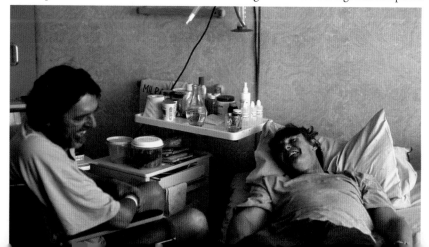

Manana the leopard: as a cub (top); with two of her cubs – all three had contracted mange, but by darting them with a powerful antibiotic we were able to save the leopards, and Manana went on to live for another thirteen years (middle); in her prime (bottom left); at sixteen years old, just before she died of natural causes (bottom right)

Filming Bongo the lion in 1994

Lakakin Sukuli, Elmon Mhlongo, Lloyd Gumede, Willie Sibuya, Michael Hackenberger, Leveres Yiamat and Moses Onossoran with Bongo the lion in Kenya

A charging male lion: a fearsome sight

Back row: Gill, Jeffrey Mhlongo, Rex Ndimande
Front row: Me, Ron the tiger, Dave Salmoni, Elmon Mhlongo and Lloyd Gumede

Swimming with a tiger in the Gariep River

No pain, no gain

A snarling tiger: an even more fearsome sight

Gill under Julie: risk and reward

What not to do! With my back turned, below a leaping tiger

Three precious gifts (clockwise): Savannah, Sean and Tao

With my sons Tao and Sean

Savannah with tiger cubs

Dave, my brother, Shanny, Bronwyn and Boyd crossing the Sand River at Londolozi (below); Princess Bronwyn sits while brother Boyd has no effect on the stuck jeep (right)

13

Manana

At Londolozi Game Reserve I am sitting with a sixteen-year-old leopard whom I call Manana, now the most-photographed leopard in the world.

Manana is the last remaining granddaughter of the Mother Leopard, the first leopard that Elmon and I habituated way back in the early eighties and nineties. The rangers at Londolozi call Manana 3:4 because of her spot pattern above the whisker line. Elmon and I call her Manana, which means 'mother' in the beautiful language of the Shangaans.

This particular morning, several game-drive vehicles have watched her unsuccessfully hunt impala.

It is getting hot and the game drives return to the comfort of the luxury lodges where the guests are accommodated.

I know that Manana's last meal was a monitor lizard and that that was two days ago, so even in the heat she may continue to hunt.

I sit down in the shade five metres away from Manana. I have done this many times – I draw energy and inspiration by being in the presence of this incredible leopard.

The film crew that is working with me moves the vehicle away to a distance of fifty metres. The air clears of the exhaust fumes and silence descends. Now it is just me and the leopard. After a short rest, Manana gets up to continue hunting. She moves away from where I am sitting, and then turns and looks back at me. Her eyes are questioning, inviting, saying to me, 'You have just one more chance to hunt with me. Now is that time.'

On impulse I get up. I have no weapon, just a camera. Manana and I move off on the hunt. It soon becomes obvious that this is not a stroll to mark territory; this is a hunt for food.

As a three-year-old leopard, Manana had contracted sarcoptic mange. She'd had two cubs at the time, and the deadly disease had been advancing rapidly. By firing three darts loaded with a strong antibiotic into Manana and her cubs, I had saved their lives and given Manana another thirteen years of life.

Is she now repaying me by taking me on this hunt, I thought to myself. I believe so.

Manana moves through dense bush. I have to remind myself that she is sixteen years old (112 leopard years) as she slips effortlessly through the bush. Manana has a low centre of gravity; with her weight distributed on four powerful legs, she glides over the ground. I am tall. Moving on two legs, I tangle; I snag; I stumble. Manana is low and unseen, while I am high and easily visible to any prey.

For an hour we hunt. Manana always stops close to a tree or bush. Here her spotted coat merges with the dappled light. She elevates herself on top of termite mounds and fallen trees. She is looking for prey ahead. I remain as low to the ground as possible as she stops to rest in the shade of a small patch of bush. I sit down outside the shade, in the heat. After a short while, she moves her position in the shade, making space for me to share it with her. This is a conscious gesture from a highly intelligent animal.

Human being and leopard sit three metres apart, contemplating life. My mind goes back to the time when an African rock python swallowed Manana's single cub. She waited for four hours for the snake to make its escape, and then she attacked, forcing the python to disgorge her cub before it slithered away. Finally Manana and I went through the grieving process and disposal of the cub together.

Does she also remember the python episode? Does she remember that I sat with her for four days as she called for her dead cub? I believe she does.

Suddenly Manana gets up and walks straight past me, brushing against me. The hunt is on. Slowly and purposefully she moves through the bush, scanning ahead, to the side and behind her. Her ears swivel, listening for the faintest sound. All her senses are operating at maximum power.

Manana communicates with me through her body, eyes and tail. If she curls her tail, it means there is game ahead; if she flicks it rapidly, the game is coming closer. At one point she turns her head and stares. This is the signal for me to get down low. It is a bewildering array of complex signs that I have to interpret.

Suddenly the impala are in front of us, moving towards us down a game path. Manana's tail whips rapidly. I freeze and crouch in the bush. She turns her head and her eyes drill into me. 'Get lower,' they command, 'lower still.' I lie flat behind her. Her eyes are riveted on the approaching impala, her concentration absolute.

An impala stops one and a half metres from the crouched leopard and some sixth sense warns it of the imminent danger. Three species – impala, leopard and human – no more than three metres apart, are frozen in a moment of time.

Then I hear the sound of an approaching jet bringing tourists to Londolozi. The jet is descending, coming in to land low over our heads. I curse the jet, fearing it will ruin the hunt. Manana seems to regard it as an advantage: she will use the sound and confusion as an opportunity to make her strike.

When the jet sound is at its loudest, the impala is distracted and Manana launches straight through the bush, going for the throat. I jump to my feet, whipping the camera left and right, hoping to catch the action. Has she caught it? Is she throttling it? I run frantically in all directions. Then it dawns on me that I am behaving like a confused impala. I could become the prey.

I can't see anything … no leopard, no impala! I sit down in a state of semi-ecstatic shock and I go through the chain of events. Did my presence on the hunt cost Manana a kill? What could I, what should I, have done differently?

In her younger days she would easily have caught the impala – I had filmed her drop onto impala and bushbuck from trees many times. I know what an incredible athlete she was.

Then the realisation dawns on me. A magnificent wild creature, a sixteen-year-old leopard, has taken me for three hours of my life on an experience I will never forget. She had nothing to gain by taking me with her. Manana had communicated with me through her body, tail and eyes, and I had tried as far as possible to obey her commands at all times. She had just taught me so much about leopard hunting in a very short space of time.

Later Manana circled around, catching a young impala as the herd came to drink at the water hole. All her experience had condensed into that hunt.

Shortly after this hunt Manana died, one month short of her seventeenth birthday. Unable to digest her food, her legs incapable of lifting her, she died with dignity.

All the staff at Londolozi observed a minute's silence for her, and the Shangaan trackers wore black ribbons on their shirts as a sign of respect. Tributes flowed in from all over the world, from guests, former rangers and all who had known and loved her.

Had we done enough for her in her old age? Had we kept our side of this incredible symbiotic relationship, which we had shared for nearly seventeen years? These were my first thoughts after she died.

I was with the Mother Leopard when she died, I was with Shingalana the lioness when she died, and I was with Julie the tigress when she came close to dying. It is a traumatic experience, to say the least. Manana is the only leopard I know of that has died of natural causes. This was a blessing and gave me some comfort.

If the Mother Leopard opened the window into the secret world of the leopard, then Manana took the leopard–human relationship to a new level and increased our understanding of leopards immensely. Manana was the first leopard in my experience to adopt a cub that was not her own. A male cub, born to her daughter Dudley River Bank Female, joined Manana and her single male cub. After she lost her own cub, Manana's adopted son stayed with her to the end of her life, killing for her, hoisting kills into trees for her and generally assisting her in her old age. Was this a deliberate strategy to help her as she got old? I believe it was.

When several of Manana's litters were killed by competing male leopards, Manana came up with an ingenious solution: she mated with all the competing males who were likely to kill her new cub if they didn't believe it to be theirs. In this way, she deceived all of them into believing that they had fathered her cub, and so gained their protection.

When I drive out into the bush at Londolozi, I go to Python Rocks and other den sites that Manana used to frequent. In these places I can feel her presence. I fully expect to find her around every bush. She will come out and gaze at me with her dark-ringed, haunting eyes. She will talk to me with her body, eyes and tail. She will say, 'You saved my life. I enriched yours.'

Manana's life is a symbol of the challenge that mankind faces. Human beings, as I have mentioned, now number close to seven billion, leopards under 100 000. As we overpopulate and dominate this fragile planet, is there a place where humans and leopards can cooperate and live in harmony? Or will humans overrun the leopard home range and take it for themselves?

At the turn of the twentieth century, there were 100 000 tigers in the forests of India; today there are barely 1 000, and India's human population is over one billion.

Will we allow the same to happen to the leopard? Will we be able to protect Londolozi and, by extension, the leopards, in the face of rising human populations? Will future generations be able to forge new relationships with ambassador leopards such as Manana? Can we build on the knowledge that the Mother Leopard and Manana gave us?

Two of Manana's daughters, Dudley River Bank Female and Notten Female, are ambassador leopards at Londolozi. Both are gentle and successful, like their mother, and both are now entering old age. These two wonderful leopards and their cubs are part of the rich legacy that Manana has left us.

Songs, poems and tributes have been written, and a major documentary for National Geographic has been made about Manana. She had power, strength, speed, beauty, courage and an incredibly trusting nature. She was loved by all; she was the Princess Diana of the leopard world. I still miss her greatly.

> If you reveal your secret life to me
> I can show the world your strength and beauty
> Caring mother that you are
> Secret hunter super star
> You will help to set me free
>
> – from 'Respect'

14

Half-Tail the Leopard

Apart from the Mother Leopard, Manana, Shingalana and the tigress Julie, several other cats have also had an impact on my life.

For seventeen years, Elmon and I travelled to the Masai Mara National Park in Kenya to film the famous annual migration of the wildebeest and the predators that preyed upon them. I had first been introduced to the Masai Mara by Warren Samuels, a Kenyan guy who had been a game ranger at Londolozi. For the first nine years, because South Africans were not allowed into Kenya at that time, Elmon and I, as mentioned earlier, travelled on Paraguayan passports that I'd been lucky enough to acquire by dubious means.

When I first visited the Masai Mara, I wanted to put up a tented camp for my film crew on the Mara River. The Masai owners of the land were very suspicious of us and demanded that I pay them a lot of money. I told them I wanted a partnership with them, but they didn't trust white people. I suggested that we buy five cows together and see how things went, plus I would pay them for their tracking work. I wasn't interested in owning cows, but having the cows meant that I retained the grass, rather than allowing the land to be ploughed for wheat. So this arrangement was good for the wildlife. In the process of tracking with us, the Masai got an idea of how our filming operation functioned.

The second year I went to the Masai Mara, the Masai arrived at the camp with a cow; they told me that they had lost one of the five cows we had bought together, so this one was to replace it.

'No, we're partners,' I replied, 'it doesn't work like that. We take the losses and the profits together.' But they insisted, saying that the herdsman had fallen asleep and a lion had taken the cow. Trust was established and so we bought ten more cows that year.

Over the many years that I was filming in the Masai Mara, we owned about 240 cows together. And we went through many experiences together. Lions killed some of our cows; some got sick and died. We drove some of them to market and sold them – we truly were partners. The Masai and I spent many hours together, sitting around waiting for cheetahs. We got to know each other really well and I was privileged to film the second and third weddings of Lakakin Sukuli, one of my partners, who is a great tracker. At his third wedding I was given quite a lot of status, which is rare for a white man.

Warren Samuels and his wife, Heather, whom he had met at Londolozi, came to help me film in the Masai Mara.

Near our camp was a beautiful rocky canyon called Leopard Gorge, with small caves and crevices that make it a perfect place for female leopards to raise their young. Leafy fig trees provide shade and good vantage points for leopards to study the plains below for suitable prey that is coming into range.

I recall the first time I saw one particularly beautiful leopard with a stunning dark coat. She was being followed by several tourist vehicles as she hunted impala. The following year, when I returned, she had lost half her tail in a fight with baboons. She now went by the name of Half-Tail the Leopard. Certainly she rivals Manana as the most photographed leopard in the world.

Unlike Londolozi, which limits the number of vehicles around a sighting to three, in the Masai Mara we often saw twelve or thirteen – sometimes as many as sixteen – tourist vehicles all packed with tourists desperate to get a picture of Half-Tail and her cubs.

Many areas in the Masai Mara do not have suitable terrain for leopards, but because Leopard Gorge has lots of den sites, the leopards compete fiercely for the prime land there. As a result, it is a good place to spot leopards. A road runs through the apparently impenetrable rugged cliffs. The drivers all knew that Half-Tail could often be found in Leopard Gorge, so somehow the tourist vehicles managed to get over the rocks and into the gorge in their quest to get a picture of Half-Tail. Sometimes they would crash into each other in their eagerness to find her, and sometimes they would get stuck. As soon as one vehicle had located her in Leopard Gorge, the word would spread like wildfire, and she would quickly be surrounded by noisy tourists clicking cameras, with flashes flashing.

Half-Tail was a celebrity cat, laid-back and tolerant of all the attention, whereas many other cats are shy and hard to find. Since the tourist vehicles don't go out at night time in the Masai Mara, at least Half-Tail had the nights to herself.

Leopard Gorge lies on the outskirts of the Masai Mara, on a ranch owned by the Masai people. The Masai are pastoralists who own sheep, goats and cattle. They don't regard a leopard as a beautiful cat that should be protected, but rather as a competitor, a killer of their domestic stock. If a leopard attacks their stock, the Masai will retaliate immediately with spears, rungus (throwing clubs) and bows and arrows.

One year when I returned to the Masai Mara, I gazed in dismay at a Masai village that had recently been built below Leopard Gorge. Instinctively I knew that it was a bad mistake and that Half-Tail's world would change dramatically. Before, she had gazed down on fleet-footed gazelle, impala and warthog; now she was looking at slow-moving sheep, goats and cows.

The Masai were not invested in tourism; they were invested in sheep, goats and cattle. Leopard and Masai were on a disastrous collision course, and I feared that Half-Tail would be the loser.

It was not long before a tribesman by the name of Oligashon reported that a leopard was, under the cover of darkness, stealing goats from his goat pen. One night Oligashon disturbed the leopard while she was in the process of killing a goat. He fired an arrow at her, but in the darkness he missed her. In the morning, Oligashon, armed with a large spear as well as a bow and a dozen arrows, followed the tracks of the leopard and found her sleeping in a tree. Because the leopard was high up in the tree, he failed to notice that half of her tail was missing. After firing half a dozen arrows at the sleeping leopard, he finally hit her in the mouth. She fell from the tree and into a dry river bed, winding herself.

As Oligashon closed in to finish off the leopard with his spear, he saw to his horror that it was Half-Tail. This leopard was a legend in the area – there was a general agreement that nobody would hurt her because she was such a tourist attraction. He could have speared her and got rid of the body, but he hesitated, and in that moment Half-Tail recovered herself and ran off.

Oligashon rushed off to the local game scouts and reported that he had shot Half-Tail with an arrow. The game scouts notified the game lodges, who immediately called a vet from Nairobi to immobilise her and remove the arrow.

When Half-Tail had been darted and was immobile, they discovered that the steel head of the arrow was embedded in the roof of her mouth. Without that intervention, there was no way Half-Tail would have been able to chew or swallow – she would certainly have starved to death.

The Half-Tail saga typifies the conflict between indigenous people in Africa and first-world visitors. To the wealthy tourist, Half-Tail was a creature of beauty to be photographed and admired. To Oligashon and the other Masai, Half-Tail robbed them of their livelihood; she was a competitor to be eliminated if possible.

After her ordeal at Leopard Gorge, Half-Tail moved north into an area already populated with several villages. Soon another Masai herdsman, Sopia, was reporting goats missing at night. The tracks indicated that it was a female leopard and, as before, Sopia was unaware that they belonged to the famous Half-Tail.

By this time Half-Tail was internationally known, having been one of the stars of the BBC television series *Big Cat Diary*, on which Warren Samuels was a cameraman. Jonathan Scott, the co-presenter of the series, had written a book about Half-Tail – *Stars of Big Cat Diary* – and she was practically a household name in the United Kingdom.

When the BBC returned to make the *Big Cat Diary* follow-up

series, there were strong rumours circulating that Half-Tail had been killed by the Masai. Jonathan Scott, the BBC, the wardens and the police investigated the matter, but the Masai steadfastly denied any knowledge of her death.

Lakakin informed me that he had heard the rumours but had no facts. I told him to take two days off to try to find out the true story of Half-Tail's death. Two days later he returned empty-handed, but suggested I go with him to the Laiboni (the local medicine man or witch doctor).

After much throwing of the bones and chanting, the Laiboni declared that Half-Tail had died of disease. I rejected this immediately, as Half-Tail was healthy and in her prime. I told Lakakin to go off for another two more days to dig deeper, offering a financial reward for information.

I said to Lakakin that I believed a Masai had killed Half-Tail and had thrown her body into the river to the crocodiles to remove all trace of her. Lakakin's response was that a Masai would never do such a thing, but that if I was right, he would give me two cows. We shook on it.

A day later, Lakakin returned and said that a man had information for me and that I should meet him at a certain tree. Lakakin gave me the appointed time and said that I should be sure to go alone. Somewhat apprehensively, I arrived at the given time and place. An hour went by. I was about to leave when out of the bush came Sopia, who was one of the owners of the camp site that I hired and, in fact, a partner of mine.

Sopia said he had been watching me from a distance to make sure that I was indeed on my own. He motioned me to follow him, checking carefully to see that we were not being observed. He took me to a tree next to the Mara River, in which I could see marks where a wire cable had cut into the bark of the tree. 'It is here that Half-Tail died,' Sopia solemnly informed me. He then told me his story.

Sopia noticed that goats were disappearing at night from his goat pens. On examining the tracks, he could tell from their size that they belonged to a female leopard. One night, he heard his dogs barking so he went outside, where he saw a leopard pulling a goat through the fence of his goat pen. He threw a spear at the leopard but missed it. He then decided to set a snare for the leopard at the hole through which he'd seen her leaving the goat pen. He attached wire cable to a large log, thinking that this would anchor the leopard when caught.

Two nights later, Sopia was again woken by his dogs barking. He rushed outside and caught a glimpse of a leopard running away, dragging the log behind her: he had caught the leopard in the snare but she had escaped. In the morning, he took two of his sons to follow her, but heavy rain in the night had washed the tracks away, and they had to abandon the search.

During the course of the morning, two of Sopia's wives went to fetch firewood. They found a leopard hanging dead in a tree, with a cable wrapped tightly around its neck. The two women told Sopia about the leopard, and he went to investigate. To Sopia's horror, he discovered that it was Half-Tail. Like Oligashon, he had had no idea that the leopard stealing his goats was the famous Half-Tail. Unlike Oligashon, Sopia told no one. He removed the leopard from the tree and threw her body into the river, where he saw her being devoured by a large crocodile, just as my sixth sense had warned me.

Sopia swore his two wives to secrecy and, although they were questioned by the police, the army and the wardens of the Masai Mara, they denied all knowledge of the killing.

I sat mesmerised by Sopia's story. When he had finished, I asked him the obvious question: 'If you have told no one up till now, why are you telling me?' Sopia reminded me of a famous lion hunt in which one Masai had been killed and three others, among them Sopia, had been badly wounded. I had taken him, bleeding profusely, to a mission hospital and thus had saved his life. He had never forgotten my kindness and was now repaying me, years later, by telling me the story of Half-Tail.

'Can I film you telling your story?' I asked.

To my amazement, he said, 'Yes, but you must not show the film to anyone for two years.' We shook hands on the deal and I asked if Lakakin could listen to the story and witness our deal. Sopia readily agreed.

I then filmed Sopia telling Lakakin the full story of Half-Tail's death. They stood under the tree where Half-Tail had died, talking in Masai. I was a little way off from them, filming. When I saw Sopia make a throwing gesture, I realised that he was telling Lakakin that he had thrown the leopard in the river. At that point, Lakakin walked across to me, shook my hand and said, 'You are a psychic, a magic man, a fortune teller, a Laiboni. I owe you two cows.'

Although I had filmed him and managed to establish the details of Half-Tail's death, I kept my deal with Sopia and, to this day, have never included the footage in any movie I have made.

Nine years later, standing in my house at Londolozi, I finally told Warren Samuels – the man who had first introduced me to the Masai Mara in Kenya – the true story of what happened to Half-Tail, the famous leopard of the Masai Mara.

15

The Tigers

In the year 2000 I acquired two tiger cubs from a friend of mine, Michael Hackenberger, from Bowmanville Zoo in Canada: a male called Ron and a female named Julie. It is with these two beautiful creatures that I started my controversial and now famous tiger-conservation experiment, which has been on the go for ten years now.

The basis of the project was the fact that no Asian country had been successful in saving the wild tiger. As mentioned earlier, in India the tiger once numbered 100 000. The number had now dropped to the thousands and was continuing to decline rapidly in the wilds. A population of 1.1 billion people in India and 1.3 billion in China – a large proportion of the earth's entire population – were competing with the tiger for space, prey and water.

My trips to India, Nepal and China had convinced me that the tiger would not be saved in Asia. My prediction has come to pass because, from the time I started the tiger project, another 4 000 tigers have been lost in the wilds.

In India's Sariska National Park and Panna National Park, in 2008 and 2009 respectively, all the tigers mysteriously disappeared, despite the wardens' claims that the tigers were there. There is no doubt in my mind that poaching, corrupt forestry officials, apathetic governments and human pressure are bringing the wild tiger to an end in Asia.

Against this backdrop, I decided to embark on an ex-situ conservation project in South Africa – this means you save the endangered species by relocating it to a country where it is possible to do so, and then, when conditions are more favourable in the country or continent from which the endangered species originated, you translocate it back. Firstly, I would make the wild tiger available to tourists, photographers, film makers and researchers, just the way we had done with the leopards at Londolozi. Secondly, I would privatise the tiger, putting wild populations of tigers in the hands of like-minded individuals instead of inefficient governments. Thirdly, I would conduct the tiger project in an area of low human density. Fourthly, I would establish the tiger sanctuary in a 'poverty pocket' of South Africa and use the tiger to attract tourists, which would create jobs for people who needed them.

When I went to fetch the two cubs from Michael Hackenberger in Canada, I persuaded a Canadian big-cat handler, Dave Salmoni, whom I'd met at Bowmanville Zoo, to come to South Africa to help me with the experiment. Dave had been well trained in the handling of large cats: in Canada and the States you have to complete five years' apprenticeship with big cats before you can become a handler. I reckoned that I could use some of the techniques with which he was familiar in preparing the tigers to be released back into the wilds. I was right: he taught us many invaluable methods that have stood us in good stead.

After exposing Ron and Julie to a variety of habitats in South

Africa's North West, KwaZulu-Natal and Northern Cape provinces, I finally acquired a beautiful piece of ground, 7 000 hectares in extent, adjacent to the Vanderkloof Dam in the Free State.

My brother, Dave, set about finding investors to buy land to increase the size of the sanctuary to an area that could hold a sizeable population of tigers. He was very successful and we increased the size of the park to 36 000 hectares on both sides of the Vanderkloof Dam in the Northern Cape and the Free State.

The park, which we called Tiger Moon, was now in a perfect position to play a major role in helping to save the declining tiger in the wilds.

The tiger was previously classified into eight subspecies, but DNA research at the Cancer Institute in Washington DC has subsequently revealed that all tigers are the same. The tiger has now been reclassified as *Panthera tigris tigris*, the Asian tiger, with just one subspecies, *Panthera tigris sumatrae*, the Sumatran tiger.

This was great news for us, because it meant that we could produce good breeding tigers from the captive population, which numbered 40 000 worldwide.

The are many successful ex-situ conservation projects around the world. Modern thinking is that developed countries have a moral obligation to help save endangered species when developing countries are not able to do so. Tiger Moon would be the first attempt to save the endangered tiger using the ex-situ conservation method. South Africa, with relatively cheap land, a strong tourist industry and an excellent conservation record, has been an outstanding location for the tiger project.

In 2002 we began fencing Tiger Moon. In order to include

the magnificent Gariep River, which runs through the core of the sanctuary, I enlisted the help of Neil McLaughlin, South Africa's leading big-game fence constructor. Neil designed a floating fence that could straddle the Gariep River.

It would now be possible for us to take tourists in a river boat up and down the Gariep River and over Vanderkloof Dam to look for tigers. We were elated.

We set about removing hundreds of kilometres of sheep fencing, gin traps, unsightly buildings and windmills. Neil McLaughlin began building the 130 kilometres of predator-proof fence to enclose the 36 000-hectare sanctuary.

Dave Salmoni, Gill and I continued with the rehabilitation of Ron and Julie, filming their daily progress as they grew from inexperienced, impatient cubs to fully fledged adult hunters.

I had constructed a hunting boma of around 150 hectares in which Ron and Julie did their early training, but we regularly took them to roam free along the Gariep River, where they hunted in the riverine bush.

The three years spent hunting with Ron and Julie were some of the most magical times of my life. To hunt with these two beautiful and intelligent creatures was an exciting, exhilarating and uplifting experience, and the knowledge we gained was truly unique. In total we concluded over 300 hunts together, of which many were successful.

One day Dave Salmoni, Andries Johnson, my film assistant, and I were hunting along the Gariep. The river was extremely full – at least 300 metres bank to bank. Dave was 100 metres ahead of me, hunting with Julie, and Andries and I were behind, hunting with Ron. I noticed on the opposite side of the river a herd of cows coming down to drink. The river was so wide that I thought nothing of it. In all the hunting I had done with other cats over the years, I had seen that they were, invariably, afraid of the water. I was soon to realise that tigers are completely different.

On noticing the cows, Ron plunged straight into the river. I gave the camera to Andries and went in after the tiger. Around my waist was wrapped the heavy chain that we used for leashing the tigers after a hunt. My plan was to leash Ron in the water and bring him back – highly ambitious to say the least. My problem was that, although I swam as fast as I could, I couldn't catch Ron. It was not that he was trying to escape me; he thought I was swimming across to join him in the hunt.

In the middle of the river my body collapsed and I briefly blacked out, rather like a car running out of petrol. Barely conscious and in danger of drowning, I managed to release the heavy chain from my waist and roll onto my back, allowing the river's current to carry me downstream.

Subsequent consultation with a doctor revealed that I had a large hydatid cyst on my liver. These cysts, which I had contracted from Shingalana the lioness, are extremely dangerous and feed off the glucose and sugar that are essential to the body. With the extreme exertion of swimming after Ron with the heavy leash around my waist, my body had simply run out of sugar and collapsed; only the icy water had kept me conscious.

Lying on my back, I drifted downstream, where Andries pulled me onto the bank. From this position I could see that the current had also pushed Ron downstream. He had landed about 200 metres from the cows and was now stalking the herd.

Dave was racing down and across the river in the boat to try to intercept Ron before he reached the cows, but Ron dodged past him and, with a huge leap, landed on the back of a cow. It takes incredible bravery and strength to leash up a male tiger that is fighting with large prey. Dave has both qualities – incredibly, he got Ron on the leash and off the cow. The cow was free to run away, but it decided to charge back, knocking Dave and Ron down.

I asked Andries to put the camera on the tripod and to fit the long 600-millimetre Canon lens so that I could record the hunt. My problem was that I was too weak to stand, so, with Andries supporting me, I rolled the dramatic shot of Ron attacking the cow that appears in the film *Living with Tigers*.

Finally, the cow, satisfied that she had dealt with her tormentors, ran off. Dave, battered and bruised, brought a dejected Ron back across the river in the boat. We returned Ron and Julie to their boma.

I immediately radioed the farmer, André Haarhoff, and told him that his cow had been badly mauled, asking him to meet us at the scene of the attack. It could not have happened at a worse time, because I was right in the middle of a delicate negotiation to buy André's farm. Although we treated the cow's wounds as best we could, three days later she died. I immediately compensated André for his loss. Thankfully, Ron's bad timing and poor public relations skills didn't cost us too much, and I was able to include André's magnificent farm in Tiger Moon.

During this time the tigers hunted and successfully captured eland, mountain reedbuck, blue wildebeest, blesbok, grey duiker, steenbok, kudu, monkey, baboon, ostrich, impala, warthog, Cape clawless otter, water mongoose, rock hyrax, porcupine and antbear, and they were even successful in catching fish in the Gariep

River. I was beginning to understand for the first time what an amazingly versatile predator the tiger is. Given suitable habitat and enough prey, the tiger can survive anywhere, provided it is protected by human beings.

In Asia the sad fact is that a tiger is worth more dead than it is alive. According to the Chinese, every part of the tiger has medicinal value, including the fat, the urine and even the whiskers, which are believed to be a cure for rheumatism.

Currently the two tiger countries China and India alone account for nearly 50 per cent of the world's human population, as mentioned earlier in this chapter. What chance does the tiger have against these formidable human densities? None.

In parts of India the tiger competes with 320 people per square kilometre for food, space and water. In China, the fourth-biggest country in the world, not a single national park has been declared to protect the tiger. In all of the traditional tiger countries in Asia, not one has a successful management blueprint to save the tiger. The Asiatic cheetah, which once roamed the entire Asian continent, is now practically extinct, and the tiger is going the same way.

When I started my tiger-conservation experiment in 2000, there were reputed to be 5 000 tigers surviving in the wilds. This number has shrunk dramatically. I am more convinced than ever that the tiger will be saved outside Asia by private individuals, not governments.

Our plan was that, when the fence was complete and Tiger Moon was fully stocked with suitable game, we would be able to support a population of thirty free-ranging, self-supporting tigers, and each year surplus wild tigers would be available for stocking other sanctuaries.

Tourists would be able to travel by jeep and boat to find and photograph the tigers. Scientists could research the tiger and its relationship with the cheetah, the leopard and, later, the lion. Local people could find jobs and receive training as game scouts, mechanics, chefs, waiters, researchers and camera assistants. This was creative conservation at its very best.

And then everything fell apart.

In March 2003, a disgruntled investor decided to take over the project. One of the tactics used was to hire eight mercenaries to harass me to try to force me off the land. Two armed mercenaries came into my house and terrorised Gill and our small kids. Highly trained, they instituted a series of intimidation tactics, including road blocks on the road to Philippolis and driving next to me pointing guns at me through the car windows.

One mercenary questioned me closely about the weight of Ron and Julie, and it was clear to me that they were planning to immobilise the two tigers in order to remove them.

I took Gill and our children from the sanctuary and hid them in a hotel nearby for safety. Dave Salmoni moved into a tent next to the tiger boma to protect Ron and Julie.

One day information came through from Philippolis that I was to be attacked by the mercenaries the following day. High on the hill above the tiger boma, Dave, Andries and I waited. Sure enough, around noon, a vehicle was spotted travelling towards the boma. I instructed Dave to take my video camera and record everything. He asked if he could carry a firearm, which I refused. I knew that if it came to a shoot-out they would cut us to pieces and then claim that they had been acting in self-defence. I told Andries to take a second car and that if a fight broke out he was to drive straight to the police station and bring the police.

The mercenaries stopped their vehicle at the tiger-boma gate and two got out, trying to see where the tigers were. The other two stayed out of sight in the vehicle. None of them saw us approaching – as they presumed we had left the land. When I greeted the first mercenary, he said he was looking for Gariep Dam, which is miles away. Dave rolled the video camera, filming me talking to the mercenaries with the tiger boma in the background, and then he filmed the registration of the vehicle. As he turned the camera onto the two mercenaries crouched in the vehicle, they both emerged from the vehicle like charging buffalo. One of them punched Dave, smashing the camera into his face and then ripping it out of his hand. The second approached me, hurling verbal abuse at me. One of the mercenaries who'd climbed out of the vehicle earlier moved behind me so that I couldn't see him, and the other one crouched behind the bonnet of their vehicle, his gun drawn.

I had no illusions about what we were dealing with. These men were well trained and they were provoking me, hoping I would retaliate. I didn't fall for the trick. I signalled to Andries to go for the police. As he drove off, one of the mercenaries threw the video camera into the moving truck.

Two things crossed my mind: the first was that the camera would be damaged, and the second was that the mercenary would surely have removed the tape that contained evidence of the attack. We later discovered, however, that the cassette was still in the camera and that the evidence was clearly visible on the cassette. The mercenaries were not so highly trained after all.

With Andries leaving the scene, the mercenaries seemed to panic and drove off at high speed. Later, when the police made an arrest and I was asked to identify the suspects, it turned out that they had been replaced by four different guys.

During the gun fight the mercenaries had made a couple of interesting comments. 'The tiger park is no longer in your hands! It's in ours!' they had said, and, 'You know what we have come for, don't you?'

I knew only too well that it was the tigers they'd come for.

That night we heard rumours that the mercenaries were returning with a film crew to film the removal of the tigers. Dave and I loaded Ron and Julie into an old Land Rover – a highly dangerous manoeuvre – and drove for eight hours, right through the night in pouring rain, to a place with holding bomas where the tigers would be safe.

I was gutted and exhausted. This had been one of the blackest days of my life. Even in the darkest moments, however, there is still place for humour. The owner of the establishment, who shall remain nameless, drew deeply on his cigarette and made the following suggestion: 'JV, do you see those two tigers in that boma over there? They have killed a few people over the years.'

'I see them,' I replied wearily.

'Let me tell the mercenaries that your tigers are here, and when they arrive to dart them I'll send them to the wrong tigers.'

'And then what?' I asked.

'And then the tigers will eat them!' he exclaimed jubilantly.

I thought that the idea was hilarious, until I realised he was absolutely serious. I could imagine the newspaper story: 'Today, in South Africa's Free State province, two tigers killed a presenter, a cameraman, a sound man, a mercenary and some investors. When asked to comment, the owner of the tigers said, "The tigers seemed to be hungry!"'

The universe has strange ways of levelling the playing fields, however. Lawyers told the Bloemfontein court that the mercenaries were not mercenaries at all, but farm managers. Shortly after this court hearing, some of the mercenaries were caught at Harare Airport on their way to the well-publicised aborted coup in Equatorial Guinea. This seemed a funny place for farm managers to turn up. They spent a year in the notorious Chikurubi Maximum Security Prison in Harare … not a pleasant experience, I presume.

After the attacks by the mercenaries, Gill took the children away to the coast at Wilderness. The trauma was so great that it took Gill five years before she was able to interact with the tigers again.

Dave Salmoni left the tigers and took up a job with Discovery Channel as a wildlife presenter.

I moved north with Ron and Julie and established Tiger Canyons in one of the most beautiful canyons in the world. Here I have bred fifteen tigers, including two white tigers. Visitors from all over the world have visited Tiger Canyons and been inspired by the project. The story of this is told in a book called *Living with Tigers*, which I am in the process of writing.

At Tiger Moon, 36 000 hectares of land now lie unproductive, the fence is in disrepair and rumours abound of poaching of the game. The dream of an ex-situ conservation project to save the tigers at Tiger Moon lies in ruins, shattered by the egos and greed of human beings. The number of tigers in the wilds in Asia has sunk to around 1 000, while 45 000 tigers pace up and down in cages worldwide.

16

The Musician

As a young boy, the highlight of my life was going to the family game farm, Sparta, for hunting trips during school holidays. At the end of every day family and friends would gather around the camp fire to tell stories and sing.

My father, Boyd, couldn't hit a single note, but he was a great storyteller; he had a knack for embellishing the facts and producing a gripping and often humorous tale.

Today I can remember every hunting story he told me as if he told it to me yesterday. My dad would go into minute detail to create atmosphere, such as, 'I carried the .416 Rigby, and Winnis was just two paces to my right with the .404, when the male lion charged out of the bush with evil intent. I knew I must clobber him now.' My dad never shot an animal; he always 'clobbered' it.

After the storytelling, my mother, Maidie, who sang very well, would take up the singing. She would go around the circle and invite each person in turn to choose a song. Then, led by her, we would all sing the song together. The storytelling and singing had a profound effect upon me, and I have enjoyed doing both at many camp fires across Africa … although I suspect that I inherited my father's musical ability rather than my mother's.

In my experience, music and storytelling are means of communicating that transcend boundaries: a good story is a good story, and a good song is a good song, no matter where you come from or what your culture is.

When we started Londolozi we continued the camp-fire tradition of singing and storytelling, and some of the happiest times of my life have been singsongs around the camp fire.

In the 1960s, singers like Bob Dylan and Joan Baez used their music to protest against the Vietnam War and other political issues. I wanted to use music to protest against what we were doing to the environment and to the earth's endangered species.

In the 1980s, the apartheid government of South Africa decided in its wisdom that it was going to mine coal in the northern part of the Kruger National Park. I immediately wrote a protest song called 'Coal Mine in Paradise' and persuaded Zimbabwean folk singer John Edmond to record it. The song got some good airtime on the local radio stations and then, suddenly, it stopped being played. Like everything else that was in any way anti-government in those days, it was banned.

I did sell two copies of 'Coal Mine in Paradise', the first to my mother and the second to Spike Milligan, who put it on a shelf with his *Goon Show* records. The song might have had some effect, however, because the South African government eventually abandoned the idea of mining coal in the Kruger National Park.

To me one of the most remarkable singers is Bob Dylan. He has recorded close to 500 songs and has made a staggering number of albums … an incredible achievement for a man who some-times sings out of key!

Many of Bob Dylan's lyrics have been strangely prophetic. He wrote: '[I] heard the roar of a wave that could drown the whole world' (from 'A Hard Rain's A-Gonna Fall') some years before the massive tsunami hit Indonesia, causing death and destruction.

He described apartheid with the following simple, yet effective, lyrics: 'Where black is the color, where none is the number … Where the executioner's face is always well hidden' (also from 'A Hard Rain's A-Gonna Fall').

When people began breeding large male lions and putting them in enclosures in order for overseas hunters to shoot them in canned lion hunts, I wrote the song 'Tell Me My Father':

> I saw the big lions, their manes were like mountains
> Waiting in cages for the hunters to come
> I heard the shots fired, saw them stagger and fall
> Now those big manes hang on American walls

After a visit to China, I was shocked by the cruelty to animals I witnessed in circuses and the filthy conditions in zoos. I wrote:

> I saw the brown monkey the cage it was tiny
> I saw the black bear the chain was so tight
> I saw the young tiger his head on a Coke tin
> I saw the chimpanzee as he rode on his bike

When the tigress Julie abandoned her three cubs and I crawled into the thick bush and discovered that two were normal-coloured and one was white, I wrote the song 'Shine a Light':

A sparkling diamond, a fragile life,
Through the tree a shaft of light
Your coat so white as fallen snow
Your eyes so blue like rivers when they flow

During the 1980s, when the Kruger National Park introduced a controversial system of capturing young elephants and culling the adults, I wrote in 'Tell Me My Father':

I saw the chopper hover low in the sky
I saw the elephants running with fear in their eyes
I saw young ones taken for circuses and zoos
Their mothers were canned into meatballs and stew

After 9/11 President Bush had a window of opportunity for world peace, when he could have engaged with the Muslim world; instead he opted for the 'War on Terror', and Tony Blair was quick to join him in invading Iraq.

I saw the president talk on the TV
He said war it was needed for our safety
Make guns and bullets, it's good for the economy
But you know he never told the children unfortunately

The planet is now facing the horrifying effects of global warming. Much of this is due to the massive destruction of the forests across the world. In Brazil, huge areas of rainforest have been destroyed so that cattle can be introduced to provide for the insatiable hamburger market. On the island of Sumatra, the Sumatran tiger is doomed because the island is being deforested so rapidly.

I saw the forest a burning, the monkeys were crying
I saw the rhinos go down, their horns were all gone
I saw the tigers a running, a running to nowhere
I saw the rivers run dry, they were scorched by the sun

After our horrendous crash in the helicopter in Luangwa I spent eight weeks recuperating in hospital, and I had plenty of time to write songs. I wrote 'Eagle in the Sky', which I dedicated to my good friend Rob Parsons, whose flying skills saved our lives that day. Part of the song is also quoted in Chapter 9.

My body is twisted and broken
Death knocks on the door, let me in
Darkness closes my senses
Will I ever see Luangwa again?

When I first went to Kenya I was stunned by the annual migration of the 1.4 million wildebeest that came from Tanzania across the Mara River. For nearly twenty years I travelled to Kenya each year to film this great spectacle. As I sat waiting for the wildebeest to arrive, I had plenty of time to research and to write. In the nineteenth century there were massive migrations of American buffalo or bison (between 50 and 60 million) and springbok in South Africa (estimated at 100 million), which, I realised during my readings in the Masai Mara, would have dwarfed the Kenyan wildebeest migration that numbered around two million.

On the southern tip of Africa
One hundred million springbok migrated
  into the Great Karoo

The farmers came with guns and traps and
    poison and above all wire fences
Where is the lion, where is the cheetah and the leopard?
Where is the Bushman?
They are gone, they are gone!

                           – from 'Rolling Thunder'

In one of the biggest crimes against humanity and the natural world, the white man killed off the buffalo across the plains of North America so that they could starve the plains Indians and obtain the grass for their cattle.

At the same time in South Africa, the lion, the leopard, the cheetah, the Cape hunting dog and the Bushman were all removed by the farmers, who wanted the land for their sheep, an exotic animal that was introduced from Europe. In the process, millions of springbok were wiped out in the name of progress and replaced with 30 million exotic sheep. In 'Rolling Thunder' I wrote:

Where are the buffalo?
They are gone
Where are the plains Indians?
They are gone too
It is one of the greatest crimes against the natural world
It is one of the greatest crimes against humanity

When the largest mammal in the world, the blue whale, was declared close to extinction and the Japanese refused to stop whaling, I wrote the song 'Mind in the Water':

I can't find you in the water
You are out of touch my sister
You seem to be a million miles away.

The sea is red and bleeding
The calves are only weaning
You close the gap and take it all away.

After filming in fourteen different countries in Africa, the
Amazon in South America, the Everglades in the United States of
America, and in China and India in Asia, I wrote 'The Cameraman', which I dedicated to all the men and women who were
leading similar lifestyles to mine.

This song is for Dereck and Beverley Joubert, David and
Carol Hughes, Alan and Joan Root, Daryl and Sharna Balfour,
Philip and Lynne Richardson, Des and Jen Bartlett, Ginger
Mauney, Dieter Plage, Simon King, Jonathan Scott, Warren
Samuels, James Boon, Peter Lamberti, Elmon Mhlongo, Lakakin
Sukuli, Karino Sukuli, Leveres Yiamat, Steve Irwin, Kim Wolhuter,
Richard Goss, Anton Truesdale, Oloff Bergh, Dave Salmoni,
John Knowles, Richard Jones, James Marshall and any others that
I may have forgotten.

He's a wildlife conservator
He's fighting for the cause
A global philosopher
Redefining nature's laws
It's a lifestyle rich in memories
He's got no money in the bank

Wild his inspiration
Put the diesel in his tank

He's in the Amazon tomorrow, Alaska for the spring
He films the icebergs melting, polar bears are leaving
The leopard stalks him forward and the cheetah runs
   with grace
Tigers fight for survival in an evolutionary race.

Elmon and I followed the Mother Leopard for fourteen years, recording nineteen of her cubs. One night, while I was filming her, I shone the spotlight on her, revealing her to the prey. I put the camera down and swore that I would never again shine a light on a leopard while it was hunting.

I wrote the song 'Respect' for all the wildlife film makers out there, inspired by the knowledge that the relationship between the cameraman and his subject must be symbiotic and respectful at all times.

Do you love me for what I am
A fellow creature trapped with you in time
Is it the photos that you take?
The money you can make?
Do you ever think of me?
Why do you shine a light into my eyes?
The prey can see me stalking in the night
You come into my place, invade into my space
Do you ever think of me?

                – from 'Respect'

After forty years of playing and singing around camp fires across Africa, I am as inspired as the day I first picked up a guitar. I have a band called The Big Cats. Zelda Kobola, a gospel singer who sings with me, has a truly beautiful voice and Druksak Andries plays drums and sings.

At Tiger Canyons I have heard fourteen different national anthems sung in one night around the camp fire. Music is truly universal.

I have always wondered why a great singer has not emerged to represent the planet. Imagine if we had an Elvis Presley or a Michael Jackson singing about conservation with images of the BP oil disaster, the endangered tiger or the New Orleans floods projected behind them.

The global human community, for its own survival, is going to have to find ways to live in a more symbiotic way with Planet Earth. Singers and musicians have enormous power and the ability to reach across religious, cultural and linguistic boundaries.

Maybe in my tenth life, if I can sing in key, I shall come back as a rock-and-roll singer representing the planet.

For now, why do I write songs and sing? Because it's good fun.

17

Goddess Gaia

When I started Londolozi back in 1973, a British scientist, James Lovelock, had postulated a theory that Planet Earth and all its components formed a self-sustaining, self-regulating ecosystem, operating as a single organism. At first many scientists around the world ridiculed Lovelock's theory, which was originally known as the 'earth feedback hypothesis' and subsequently named the 'Gaia hypothesis' or 'Gaia theory'. Today, however, as Mother Earth begins to flex her muscles in protest against mankind's abuses, the Gaia hypothesis has begun to gain support from even the most cynical of scientists, who have been forced to admit that James Lovelock has been right all along.

Modern man understands and acknowledges that many cultures inhabited this planet before he did. The dinosaurs lived on the earth for millions of years and then they disappeared. Modern man knows that he is a newcomer to this planet. He is slowly coming to realise that his actions will have far-reaching repercussions on Planet Earth and on mankind itself.

Human beings are intelligent – highly intelligent … or are they?

How is it that a species that has landed a man on the moon, can fly a jet aircraft at the speed of sound and can talk across the length of the planet on a cellphone will commit millions of dollars per minute to death, destruction and war?

When the Falklands, a tiny island belonging to Britain, threatened the British Empire in 1982, the prime minister of the time, Margaret Thatcher, a woman and a mother, had no hesitation in going to war. After 9/11 the then president of the United States, George W Bush, had the opportunity to engage with the Muslim world, but he chose war instead. The 'War on Terror' has now cost billions of dollars and the cost to the environment is incalculable.

I am constantly amazed at the tiger. Weighing no more than one kilogram at birth, the tiger cub is born blind and helpless. Within thirty days the cub is four times heavier than it was when it was born. At twelve months it can catch and kill a prey species equal to its own weight; at twenty-four months it can catch and kill an animal three times its own weight; and at thirty-six months a tigress can produce and raise cubs of her own.

By the time a human female is ready to give birth to her first child, the life of the tigress is almost over. How is it that this slow-moving, flat-footed, weak primate now dominates the entire globe and affects every facet of the earth's ability to self-regulate?

As I have noted, the tiger population of the world is down to around 1000 in the wild, while the human population is presently approaching seven billion. Like tens of thousands of other endangered species, the tiger simply cannot compete with human beings.

I have a T-shirt that bears the legend, 'Save the tiger and you save the forest, the rivers, the birds and insects and indeed the entire pyramid of life'. Modern man has failed to understand that saving the forests is not only essential to the future of the tiger, but vital to his own survival as well.

The forests of the world are its very lungs. If we destroy the lungs, the planet will die, and if the planet dies, the human cancer that inhabits it dies with it.

But will Gaia, the earth goddess of the ancient Greeks, allow one species to kill her and millions of species with her? No, Planet Earth will adapt to her new set of circumstances. She will ensure her own survival at the expense of her most voracious and notorious predator – human beings.

She has more than enough tools at her disposal: fire, flood, heat, cold, drought, disease, volcano, earthquake, tsunami, hurricane and tornado, to name a few.

Over the last decade she has flexed her considerable muscle and delivered a warning to modern man. Has he responded; does he understand; can he turn it around? Not according to James Lovelock.

People often ask me why I spend long periods of time on my own in the company of big cats. 'Do you prefer cats to people?' is the most common question I am asked. The answer is no. Like every normal human being, I am a social primate. My survival and happiness are closely linked to the love and support of my family and friends.

With the exception of lions, who live in prides, the big cats are solitary and independent, responsible only for themselves. When you interact with big cats, they communicate directly with you. If they are happy, they chuff; when they are threatened, they growl and snarl; when they are angry, they bite and kill.

I admire this directness and honesty; I understand it.

Humans are different: they are primates and have a huge capacity to deceive. They will shake hands with you while they have a weapon concealed upon them. They will smile when treachery is their real motive. Greed and the desire for power are strong in primates. This might explain why this ostensibly intelligent super-ape is unable to respond to Planet Earth's warning signals.

Of the nearly seven billion people presently inhabiting the earth, more than half are not existing in a symbiotic relationship with Gaia. Living in megacities, they are detached from the cause and effect of earth's natural systems.

Therefore, when Al-Qaeda flew aeroplanes into the World Trade Center in New York City, modern man immediately responded in an aggressive way.

I once watched two baboons cooperate to kill a gazelle fawn. They did not share the spoils – the bigger baboon took the whole kill for himself. Similarly, with humans, the greed – the desire for power and dominance over earth and fellow species – overrides the nurturing and sharing impetus and the harmony in all of us.

Can modern man evolve into a cooperative, harmonious super-ape? I can't say. Maybe after Gaia has dealt him some massive physical, psychological and emotional blows and greatly reduced his numbers he will rise as a species that recognises that, like all other species, he must obey the laws of nature.

I have another T-shirt that reads, 'The world is waiting for a new direction, one based on the laws of nature'. I believe this to be true.

* * *

Thank you for sharing my story. This book has been written in the hope that modern man can find a way to live in harmony with his fellow creatures, and that future generations will be able to see a wild tiger stalking through the jungles of Asia, a leopard hoisting its kill at Londolozi and a cheetah running down a gazelle in the Masai Mara.

To all of mankind and to the children of the future, I say tread lightly on Mother Earth and find ways to live in harmony with her.

Filmography

Living with Tigers | 2003
Two-hour wildlife documentary

Living with Tigers tells the story of how the two pioneer tigers Ron and Julie learn to hunt in Africa. John Varty and Dave Salmoni go on an extraordinary adventure for four years as they conduct this incredible hunting experiment with the two magnificent cats, who learn to stalk, to hunt and to associate hunting with food. In one hunt, Ron and Julie capture seven blesbok and springbok. Ultimately the tigers turn into fine hunters.

Animal Powers | 2000
52-minute wildlife documentary

In a refreshing departure from the usual angle on wildlife, this film explores the ancient, mystical and sacred relationship with nature and animals that humans have enjoyed for aeons. *Animal Powers* investigates the symbolism surrounding certain animals in different tribes in southern Africa. It reveals ancient and current perspectives on African animals and people's relationships with them over thousands of years. Exquisite footage, combined with little-known myths, legends and facts, creates a documentary of entrancing entertainment.

Wet and Wild | 2000
52-minute wildlife documentary

Maputaland, South Africa – part paradox, part paradise, unrivalled in biological diversity: the story of Africa today. This is the land of the Amatonga – the people of the dawn. The wetlands are part of a distinct geographical entity of 8 000 square kilometres, supporting fifteen different vegetation communities and seven distinct ecosystems. It is a wilderness as diverse as the creatures that inhabit it. It is both very wet and very wild.

Londolozi's Africa | 2000
53 one- to four-minute interstitials

The fillers of *Londolozi's Africa* are all theme based, ranging from individual species to environmental concerns; some are educational and all are entertaining. They do have one overall driving factor: they are unashamedly pure-bred African products. They have been designed to reflect Africa today, vibrant, creative, exciting and mysterious.

Sense & Scentability | 2000
52-minute wildlife documentary

Have you ever wondered why one animal would choose to eat flesh while another eats vegetation? To find out, this film travels back forty million years to the first true carnivores to investigate the reason for their taste for meat. At the same time, it looks at the ungulates to see why they choose to eat vegetation. *Sense & Scentability* is an easy-to-digest comparison of the senses of carnivores and ungulates, following the development of these two lines of mammals to the present.

Jamu (re-edit) | 2000
52-minute wildlife documentary

Filmed in the Luangwa Valley, Zambia, this documentary is an edited version of the two-part docu-drama *Jamu – The Orphaned Leopard.*

The re-enacted scenes have been removed, leaving behind the natural interaction between Jamu and John Varty.

The Brotherhood | 2000
52-minute wildlife documentary

Deep in the heart of South Africa's lowveld roam the Selala pride. Two large males, somewhat past their prime, control four females and their offspring. Life for them is remarkable only in that it is normal. Yet it has not always been this simple. *The Brotherhood* is a powerful story of generations, starting with the lions' conflict with man and their battle against invading males from other territories, and ending with an unlikely partnership between man and the pride.

The Tracker | 1999
52-minute cultural/wildlife documentary

Elmon Mhlongo, once a tracker, now a cameraman and actor, shares his experiences, conservation views and stories through his camera lens. *The Tracker* is a 'hands-on' inside look at life in the bush and provides intriguing insights into the world of nature from the Shangaan perspective.

Savage Instinct | 1999
52-minute wildlife documentary

Are prey species evolving to become smarter and more intelligent than their predecessors? If so, predators must also be evolving in order to remain in the survival race. Are the lion, the leopard and the cheetah faster and stronger than they were a thousand years ago? These are some of the thought-provoking hypotheses probed in *Savage Instinct*.

Ambush in Paradise | 1999
52-minute wildlife documentary

As the East African plains dry after the summer rains, the horizon becomes blurred with vast herds as they head north into the Masai Mara in Kenya in search of grazing and water. Several weeks later, the great herds amass along the Mara River, but a deadly flotilla of some of the largest and most experienced of Africa's crocodiles awaits the herds at the crossing points as they plunge into the river. It is this unpredictable and volatile river that sets the stage for extraordinary life-and-death dramas.

Return of the Kings | 1999
52-minute human/animal docu-drama

Thousands of animals are being introduced into the Tswalu Reserve in the Kalahari – bankrupt farmland, which is presently being returned to its original state. Along with these animals come Nkosi, Duma and Lozi – three cheetah cubs that have been hand-reared in this vast reserve of red sand dunes and expansive blue skies. Follow the journeys of these three cubs on their road to adulthood.

Jamu – The Orphaned Leopard | 1999
Two-part 52-minute human/animal docu-drama

Jamu is left orphaned at two weeks of age after her mother is killed in a snare. Under the tender care of John Varty and his team she survives severe dehydration and slowly begins to explore her world. We witness the trials and tribulations of rearing this leopard cub and preparing her for life in the pristine wilderness of Zambia's Luangwa Valley.

A Secret Life | 1999
Two-part 52-minute human/animal docu-drama

Lula, a leopard, gives birth to a litter of cubs at Londolozi Game Reserve. John, Elmon and Gillian visit the den site and film the cubs and Lula when she returns to suckle them. We become involved in Lula's journey of survival and observe how she copes with adversity. Ultimately we witness Lula and the leopards of Londolozi deal with nature's strict rules of life and death.

Survival on the Savannah | 1999
52-minute wildlife documentary

The dry season approaches and the buffalo herds move from the grasslands to the river. Dramatic sequences reveal the relationship between buffalo and lion as the film investigates these two giants of the African savannah. *Survival on the Savannah* critically evaluates the causes of their rapidly diminishing habitat through overpopulation and the ever-expanding beef industry.

Perfect Mothers, Perfect Predators | 1998
52-minute wildlife documentary

Two of Africa's greatest predators, the cheetah and the leopard, raise their cubs in the Masai Mara, Kenya, teaching them to hunt and fend for themselves. The cubs watch and try to mimic their mothers' stealth and cunning, joining in on the hunts until they reach independence.

Brothers in Arms | 1998
52-minute cultural/wildlife documentary

The Masai are warlike, loyal, brave and colourful nomadic tribesmen who live on the great plains that stretch between Kenya and Tanzania. Their land is an integral part of the great wildebeest migration, one of the natural wonders of the world. *Brothers in Arms* documents the lives of three brothers, and through their eyes we witness the Masai culture and how change has affected the Masai people's traditional way of life.

River Dinosaur – A Crocodile Safari in Africa | 1998
52-minute wildlife documentary

Of all the species of crocodile that inhabit the planet, the Nile crocodile is one of the most notorious. John and Elmon follow this much-maligned creature on a wild safari across South Africa, Zambia and Kenya. With reptilian intelligence, the crocodile has devised cunning techniques to catch wildebeest and zebra as they come to drink or cross Kenya's Mara River. Although supreme in water, the crocodile must occasionally compete with lion and hyena as these land predators manoeuvre the migrating herds into the river.

The Mating Game | 1998
52-minute wildlife documentary

The species that survive today are those that have been able to pass on their genetic formulae to the next generation and so perpetuate their species. How do the opposite sexes find a mate, court and copulate? Some of them have lengthy, elaborate courtship systems; some have brief interludes. The only criteria are success and survival of the species.

Cycle of the Seasons | 1997
52-minute wildlife documentary

The Masai Mara in Kenya is an integral part of the Serengeti ecosystem and one of Africa's greatest wildlife sanctuaries. Adjoining the Mara River is the Musiara Marsh, which plays host to a myriad species. Animals are drawn to this green oasis from the far Serengeti plains. This film follows hordes of wildebeest and zebra as they move through the game reserve on their spectacular annual migration.

Living with Leopards series | 1997
Three-part 45-minute human/animal docu-drama;
94-minute human/animal docu-drama

For fourteen years at Londolozi Game Reserve, John Varty, Gillian van Houten and Elmon Mhlongo followed and observed the magnificent Mother Leopard, filming and recording details of her life as she raised nine litters of cubs. One night she is fatally mauled by lions, leaving two orphaned cubs. The cubs, called Little Boy and Little Girl, are adopted by their human friends, raised and finally released into the wilds of the Luangwa Valley in Zambia.

Shingalana series | 1996

Three-part 52-minute human/animal docu-drama;
90-minute human/animal docu-drama

Shingalana – the 'little lion' abandoned at birth – is adopted by John Varty, Gillian van Houten and Elmon Mhlongo. Shingi enriches their lives but is torn between her devotion to her human pride and her natural instinct to return to her own kind. It is a journey filled with adventure and excitement as Shingalana encounters other animals that share her world and learns the skills that will prepare her for the wild.

Super Hunts – Super Hunters | 1995

52-minute wildlife documentary

We take a closer look at the super-predators, their hunting techniques and the cameramen who follow them to capture that elusive, ultimate, perfect kill. *Super Hunts* illustrates, with the aid of computer graphics, each of the animals' unique styles of hunting, specifically developed to suit the habitat in which they live.

Savannah Cats | 1995

52-minute wildlife documentary

In the savannah grasslands of Africa, two great cats have evolved to hunt their prey successfully – the cheetah and the lion. Although they employ totally different hunting methods, both are successful in their own right. *Savannah Cats* explores the different social structures and the techniques used by the females to raise their young. The film offers a plea to use ecotourism as a means of preserving the magnificent grasslands in which these two predators thrive.

Hyaena – The Greatest Opportunist | 1994

52-minute wildlife documentary

The survival of the spotted hyena has been adversely affected by the prejudices of man. This formidable predator has long been misunderstood, and although it is rated as one of the five super-predators, today it is still depicted as a cowardly, skulking scavenger. This film presents the much-maligned predator in a different light.

Troubled Waters | 1993
52-minute wildlife documentary

Migrating herds of zebra and wildebeest run the gauntlet of the crocodile-infested Mara River in Kenya. Gazelle are massacred as they blindly follow their lead female into the treacherous water. The crocodile's perfect adaptation to its aquatic environment is revealed through underwater sequences. *Troubled Waters* draws our attention to the integral role rivers play in our ecosystem and shows how rapidly these life-support systems are failing.

The Super Predators | 1993
52-minute wildlife documentary

Filmed over three years at Londolozi Game Reserve in South Africa and Kenya's Masai Mara, *The Super Predators* captures extraordinary scenes of predators hunting and killing. Included is a plea to the world's most notorious predator, man, to work towards a closer partnership with nature for our mutual benefit and survival.

Running Wild | 1992
108-minute feature film

Twelve years in the making, *Running Wild* is the story of two orphaned leopard cubs, the man who saves them and the woman who wants to bring their story to the world. It stars Brooke Shields as a fledgling documentary film maker and John Varty as the enigmatic conservationist whose love for a female leopard leads him to violate his jungle code and rescue her two cubs. John's intense concern for these animals ultimately leads to his struggle to find a home for the orphaned cubs once they are ready to be set free.

Swift and Silent | 1992
52-minute wildlife documentary

John Varty and Elmon Mhlongo continue their adventures into some of the most remote, endangered and inhospitable regions of the South American Amazon Jungle, the Masai Mara grasslands of Kenya and the bushland of southern Africa. *Swift and Silent* examines these threatened habitats and compares the physical, behavioural and hunting differences between the spotted predators that exist there – the jaguar, the leopard and the cheetah.

The Bush School series | 1991
Thirteen-part 45-minute educational/wildlife documentary
for children

Environmental awareness is now an essential part of every child's education. In *The Bush School* series six young children investigate the fascinating elements of wildlife and nature, and receive in-depth instruction on a variety of interesting subjects – from biological facts to animal-behavioural patterns – from which humankind can learn. Topics covered include nature's relationships, feeding cycles, animal defences, camouflage and flight, as well as a diversity of individual animals.

Winged Safari | 1989
Two-part 52-minute wildlife documentary

Game ranger Lex Hes travels over 20 000 kilometres and crosses three continents to follow the migration route of the white stork. The film documents the views of many ornithologists, scientists and birdwatchers as it witnesses the escapades of Lex on his wildlife safari across nine countries. Yet behind the humour and the beauty of the journey lies the disturbing message that our planet is in serious decline.

Leopard – Prince of Predators | 1987
52-minute wildlife documentary

The viewer is transported into the world of Africa's mightiest, most elusive and least understood predator – the leopard. The film examines the natural balances and pressures that prevail in the wild and observes a world that can often turn the hunter into the hunted.

The Silent Hunter | 1986
52-minute wildlife documentary

The Silent Hunter took cameraman John Varty five years to film. It is the story of how he and his trusted friend Elmon Mhlongo develop a unique association with a family of wild leopards. Contained in the film is a vast store of information about one of Africa's most elusive predators, a silent, devastatingly successful hunter – the leopard.

The Crossover | 1984
52-minute cultural/wildlife documentary

The Crossover explores the Shangaan culture and traditions as John Varty and Lynne Eayrs spend a year with Elmon Mhlongo and his family. Through the eyes of Africa's indigenous people we learn the Shangaan hunter-gatherer's viewpoint on the realities of conservation. Life-and-death sequences include crocodile and venomous-snake attacks, and close encounters between man and Africa's major predators.

Focus on Africa | 1984
26-minute wildlife documentary

Set in Londolozi Game Reserve, *Focus on Africa* offers a unique insight into the social and hunting behaviour of Africa's most noble predator – the lion. Ian Thomas, a wildlife photographer, shares some of his techniques of photographing animals in the wild. His tracker, Phineas Mhlongo, imparts his unique bush and tracking knowledge. Together with John Varty, they capture the magic and mystery of Africa.

Children of Africa | 1983

52-minute human docu-drama

In the wild and untamed wilderness of Londolozi Game Reserve, two young adventurers discover the secrets of Africa's animal kingdom and learn that the natural world can be a cruel and harsh one as animals fight for survival. Young audiences are able to identify with the two young characters as they provide an absorbing glimpse into a world of wildlife that is fast becoming a rarity. The adult viewer is asked to consider what the future holds for the children of Africa.

Index